The Complete Book
Of African Violets

BY HELEN VAN PELT WILSON

M. Barrows and Company, Inc · Publishers · New York

Copyright 1951 by Helen Van Pelt Wilson. Manufactured in the United States of America by The Cornwall Press, Inc., Cornwall, N. Y. Designed by Stefan Salter.

First Printing, September 1951
Second Printing, November 1951
Third Printing, April 1952

To
The African Violet Society of America, Inc.
With Gratitude
For Their Energy and Good Works

Contents

	PAGE
So Many Thanks	11

CHAPTER		
1.	To Make Them Bloom	17
2.	New Plants from Old	47
3.	Planned Parenthood	61
4.	From Seed to Flower	78
5.	Greenhouse Wisdom	86
6.	Evil Elements—Pest and Disease	112
7.	Are You a Joiner?	136
8.	Show Business and Judging	144
9.	Wrap It Up	159
10.	The Species—A Fascinating History	169
11.	Infinite Variety	184
	Saintpaulia Language	234
	Index	239

List of Illustrations

IN COLOR

Handsome Trio   FACING PAGE 128
    Amazon Purple Prince
    Snow Prince
    Tinari's Pink Luster

    FRONTISPIECE
Saintpaulia Window Garden (Courtesy of *Farm Journal*)
    Top: Bicolor, Blue Girl, Blushing Maiden Supreme, DuPont Lavender Pink
    Center: White Lady, Blue Boy, Pink Beauty, Blue Chard, Red Head
    Bottom: Red Head, Bicolor

Parade of Varieties   BETWEEN PAGES 128 AND 129
    Lady Geneva
    Pink Beauty
    Violet Beauty
    Sailor Girl, Variegated
    Red King

LIST OF ILLUSTRATIONS

Neptune BETWEEN PAGES 128
Apollo AND 129
Mauve Fringette
Amazon Blue Eyes
DuPont Lavender Pink
Tear Drop
Fantasy
Helen Wilson
White Fringette
Tinari's America

DRAWINGS

	PAGE
How to Repot a Plant	41
Methods of Propagation with Leaves	52, 53
Variegated Type, DuPont Lavender Pink	57
Structure of a Flower	69
How to Hand-Pollinate	71
Seeds and Seedlings	81
How to Wrap a Plant or Leaves for Mailing	166, 167
S. ionantha, Species (1895)	171
S. diplotricha, Species	177
S. ionantha, Species (Modern)	180
S. ionantha, a Spooned Type	185
Neptune, with Spooned Foliage	187
Orchid Beauty, Hanging-Basket Type	189
Saintpaulia Color Chart	190, 191
Typical Leaf Forms	194
Amethyst	197

LIST OF ILLUSTRATIONS

	PAGE
Bicolor	199
Blue Bird	200
Blue Boy	201
Blue Boy Supreme	203
Blue Chard	204
Blue Eyes	205
Blue Girl	207
Double Blue Boy	209
DuPont Blue	211
DuPont Lavender Pink	213
Norseman	215
Orchid Beauty	217
Orchid Beauty (Detail)	219
Pink Beauty	221
Ruffles	223
S. ionantha (Detail)	225
Sapphire	226
Starlight	227
Viking	229
White Lady	231

So Many Thanks

When in August, 1947, I finished writing my first book on the African violet, it did not occur to me that I would be doing a brand new one on the same subject not four years hence, and with two big revisions of the first book in between. But this African violet is a fast woman, if I may say so, knowing her as well as I do. She is not only forever extending herself so that last year's "complete" variety list is just about as up to date today as yesterday's bargains, but her vagaries are so enormous as to invite continuous investigation and research—all of which I hope to keep recorded. So instead of a 1951 revision, as planned, I have written a new 1951 book.

Only a few short sections of text and Leonie Hagerty's lovely line drawings have been retained from the earlier work. They seemed too fine to be shut away where no one would see them any more. To the originals, six more have been added. The new ones cover potting, pollinating, plant structure, seed sowing, and the wrapping of leaves and plants for mailing.

This time there is color, 29 plants in their true and lovely hues. The pictures on the jacket and in the portfolio were taken by Noel Boghetti of Hatboro, Pennsylvania, who will tell you with a grin that I wouldn't even let him stop to smoke, so press-

SO MANY THANKS

ing was the schedule to get the wealth of new saintpaulia information quickly into print.

The frontispiece photograph of the window garden is used through the courtesy of *Farm Journal*.

All the beautiful saintpaulias who sat for their portraits were supplied to the studios by the Tinaris of Bethayres, Pennsylvania, and Fischer Flowers of Atlantic City, New Jersey. Those in the window garden came entirely from the Tinaris, and I am indebted beyond words to Anne Tinari for her wonderful assistance—and humor—through the whole hard-working schedule of photography at the Boghettis. I am so pleased too that I was permitted to see the new Tinari's Pink Luster, not even in commerce at the time the cover picture was taken.

Many, many people have contributed to the information in this book. With the permission of the Editor, I have drawn freely on material published in *The African Violet Magazine*. I know you share with me appreciation for the excellent work done by the Neil Millers on mite and nematodes, by the Warren Gottschalls on thrips, and by Evan Roberts and Harvey Cox on the species. I am also grateful to Inez Kelley for ferreting out the quarantine regulations of the United States and Canada, to Annette Sculley for her symposium on variegation, to Ruth Dahnke for her clarification of patented plants and other contributions to our knowledge, to Rosa Peters on Fermate, to Fay Stillwell for her reports on fluorescent light, to Bess Hardy of the *Dayton Daily News* for her excellent ideas on organizing clubs, and to Ruth G. Carey, Chairman of the Committee on Show Preparation and Judging. I also want to thank Charles W. Fischer, Jr., Frank Tinari, and Ernest Chabot, author of *Green-*

house Gardening for Everyone, for careful consideration of my material about gardening under glass, and Dr. A. W. Dimock of Cornell University for reading the discussion on disease.

My thanks are also poured forth in profusion to Alma Wright, who willingly added to her schedule of shows, speeches, and quarterly-magazine publication, the task of reading this entire book manuscript and giving me the benefit of her most knowledgeable criticism.

I wish to thank my colleagues at Barrows, and particularly Nedda Casson Anders, who carried the burden of much of my correspondence and editorial work, so that I might be free long enough to write another book on the subject of your admiration, and mine—the African violet.

Finally I wish to pay tribute to the late H. Tanner Olsen, President of M. Barrows and Company, Inc., who had the faith to publish a book on saintpaulias at a time when the subject was generally unknown in the book world, who gave me the privilege of constant revision, and then the opportunity to write a new book, when I felt a fresh discussion was important. He will long be remembered by all his authors for his vision, generosity, and ethical dealings. This is the first Barrows' book to be published after his death on July 5, and there is sadly lacking the fun and excitement of the usual launching, but for comfort there remains his confidence in the subject and in me.

HELEN VAN PELT WILSON

Westport
Connecticut
June, 1951

… THE COMPLETE BOOK OF AFRICAN VIOLETS

CHAPTER ONE

To Make Them Bloom

*God made the flowers to beautify
The earth and cheer man's careful mood:
And he is happiest who hath power
To gather wisdom from a flower.*

WILLIAM WORDSWORTH

The African violet is a born internationalist. Wherever I have traveled, east, west, north, or south, I have found it thriving on window sills or filling colorful greenhouses. In England, France, Denmark, Norway, and especially Sweden, the purples are seen everywhere. Modest as it appears, the saintpaulia gets around, and today is the most popular houseplant in the world.

Growers tell of requests for plants from the far places of the globe. Besides the countries of Western Europe, they receive letters from Egypt, India, Japan, Australia, even the land of origin—East Africa. In this hemisphere, they ship successfully from Alaska to the Canal Zone, and have a lot of pleasure doing it. We agree with the nurseryman who said, "If there were more violet fans, there would be less trouble in the world." Certainly saintpaulia growing is a delightful occupation, and sure to promote personal contentment.

As one who loves this plant, I feel I must admit that its fatal fascination lies in an alluring personality, not an agreeable disposition. When it comes to flowering, it can be stubborn indeed. Yet difficulties apparently do not affect popularity. Hundreds of varieties are now eagerly sought by thousands of fanciers, many of whom repeatedly ask, "How can I make them bloom?" One expert at a show in Rochester, New York, answered the question 500 times, or tried to, for the answer is necessarily complex.

TRUTH ABOUT FLOWERING

Flowering is not dependent on some trick or magic formula, but is the result of a number of factors which add up to good health for violets—and hence bloom. Even successful commercial growers do not entirely agree on culture, and offer somewhat contradictory advice. In evaluating this, we must remember that we are not dealing with one type of plant, but with several.

In East Africa, its native place, the saintpaulia appears in a number of species, not just the familiar ionantha. It grows and thrives between rocks and in rich earth, "in wooded places" and "in the primeval forest . . . in shady situations." Some plants have been discovered in East African highlands, where temperatures fall as low as 40 degrees F.; others, as ionantha, grow in coastal areas, where the *average* temperature is 80 degrees. Who can say today what hereditary influences are affecting your plants—that of the cold, rocky mountain top or the tropical lowland?

Despite their vagaries, perhaps due to a mixed heritage, many

TO MAKE THEM BLOOM

of us have found certain methods of saintpaulia culture satisfactory enough to recommend. As you consider these, keep in mind that you should have different expectations of bloom for different varieties. A realistic approach means much less disappointment. The duPonts will have larger flowers, and fewer of them at longer intervals than the free-flowering, smaller-blossomed Blue Boy. Amazons and Supremes put on a more brilliant but less constant show than the older standard varieties, such as Viking and Mentor Boy, which may "always be in bloom." Newer varieties that have proved to be very good bloomers include: Violet Beauty, Red King, Snow Prince, Double Neptune, Dixie Rose, Orchid Crinkles, Fantasy, Blue Butterfly, and Mulberry Girl.

Young plants obviously will not put on the show of large mature specimens. Some rest period between heavy periods of color is also normal, but resting should be a matter of days or weeks at the most, not of months. However, plants moved from greenhouse to living room might sulk that long, since your average conditions may be a far cry from the ideal ones they have been enjoying. And obviously, any variety may be a shy bloomer if not well looked after.

So with reservations as to varieties and age let us look at the cultural factors which produce flowers.

LIGHT

Give your violets all the light, and as much sunshine as they will stand. This will never be a summer flood, but morning sun in winter is not harmful. Sunshine produces flowers, but too much affects foliage adversely, turning it yellow, burning the margin of leaves, and causing malformation of leaf and flower. Seek the happy medium. Only if you have plants that appear healthy, but just won't set a bud, try the shock of full sunlight in summer. It has worked. Even if it does bleach the foliage a little, it may start plants blooming. I believe we have often been too chary of sunshine. Beautiful dark green foliage and no flowers usually are an indication of too little light.

Violets may be grown at any window in your house that is well lighted, not darkened by trees, and at any sunny window, where the brightness is somewhat diffused or where plants can be set back a little from the sun. If you wish to use south windows, temper the brilliance of late spring and summer there with a thin curtain or a Venetian blind, the slats tilted upward during sunniest hours. Let your violets tell you what light they want. In a week you can read the answer "too much sunshine" in off-color leaves. If you have a photographic light meter you can test the amount of light and discover what is best.

At the 1949 Convention of the African Violet Society, Mr. H. G. Harvey made this suggestion: "A proper location . . . as measured with a photographic light meter by the incident light method, will give a maximum reading of not over 60 foot-candles, and an average value for an 8-hour period of 15 and 30."

Cornell University advises 1000 foot-candles minimum, 1500 foot maximum. Without measuring we know that the stronger the light plants can safely endure, the deeper the color tones and the greater the number of flowers. Be sure to keep turning your plants so that all growing parts will receive an equal amount of light. A quarter turn, clockwise, once a week is fine; oftener if you are growing show plants.

MORE BLOOM THE FLUORESCENT WAY

The effect of light has been proved by the fine response of violets to increased hours of light and the greater brilliance of it, possible when they are grown under a fluorescent fixture. In fact, for getting violets to bloom and bloom, nothing seems to beat exposure to fluorescent light. In some cases, results rival those of greenhouse culture, and it has even been said, *sotto voce* of course, that "I wish I could exchange my lean-to greenhouse for a big fluorescent set-up." A greenhouse obviously offers many advantages besides adequate lighting, but if you can't have one, put up a 50-inch fluorescent fixture in your living room, or even in your cellar, if your winter temperatures there won't go often below 60 degrees F. Use two 40-watt daylight bulbs, keep the light on 14 hours, off 10, and be prepared to cheer.

A couple of feet below the light, place table or stepladder plant stand. If the top shelf is a foot nearer the light, the location will still be all right for young plants which are being encouraged to start blooming. It seems to be too close for mature plants, which begin to "look down."

The usual fixture has a reflector of about a 12-inch diameter. If you can get an 18-inch reflector—with the same two 40-watt bulbs—it will permit more plants to come within the very adequate range of light. You can have a time switch attached to the fixture so you won't have to mind it. If the cellar offers the only possible place for a fluorescent light, you can produce more and larger flowers down there for display in the living and dining rooms upstairs. Unlike the effect of moving from greenhouse to living room, the change from fluorescent to daylight seems unnoticed. Plants don't miss a beat!

TEMPERATURE

Despite the 40- to 80-degree F. tolerance of their ancestors, modern saintpaulias are no more likely to thrive under the conditions their pioneer forefathers endured than we are to enjoy the Pilgrims' hardships. In the house, African violets like it fairly warm, a day temperature up to 75 degrees F., best at 70 to 72 degrees. Their liking for heat is another good reason for popularity. Too many lovely houseplants prefer 60 degrees, and what human being is comfortable at that?

A night temperature of 60 to 65 degrees F. is good. There should be about a 10-degree drop after dark, as in nature, when the sun goes down. But watch out for temperatures below 60 degrees. Such coolness could be an answer to non-flowering. At night in bitter winter weather, slip thicknesses of newspaper between your violets and the window glass or keep the shade or Venetian blind drawn. And if you have a greenhouse, watch out for extremes, especially in spring and fall. Temperatures soaring to 90 degrees in the daytime and dropping to 50 at night do not promote bloom.

A "BUOYANT" ATMOSPHERE

A fresh atmosphere is essential for flowering. Even in cold weather, try to avoid closeness. It's no better for plants than for you. Maintain a "buoyant" atmosphere. It's an inspiration to budding. Indirect ventilation from an adjoining room is the safest plan. In most dwellings where doors to the outside are frequently in use, the matter of fresh air takes care of itself. If your violets are in an apartment, have a "program" of ventilation, as greenhouse men do. A good airing the first thing in the morning, and again in mid-afternoon if you are equal to both, will promote health, and so flowering. Try closing the room where the plants are and opening a window in an adjoining room for half an hour or less, depending on weather. After you close it, open the doors of the plant room, and the new air, not too cool now, will circulate refreshingly.

However, if gas is escaping from cookstove or heater, fresh air won't protect your plants from poisoning. Dark, almost-black, buds falling prematurely, yellowing foliage are possible indications of gas poisoning, as well as non-flowering. Gas may seep out in quantities too minute for you to notice, but enough to make your violets sick. If there is any possibility of this kind of trouble, why not have your gas company make an inspection? This is done free of charge.

PROPER WATERING

One vital factor to flowering is water in adequate, just-right amounts. Yet I can give you no rule as to quantity, only as to temperature. *Water must be of room temperature.* You don't have to check it with a thermometer, but take care that it is not cold, but tepid. If the water is 10 degrees above or 10 degrees below room temperature, leaf spotting may occur, even though not one drop of water touches foliage. Cold water particularly has a shocking effect, and nothing could be more of a detriment to bloom than a thorough chilling of the roots. The room-temperature rule applies also to sprays, which must be mixed with warm water, and to syringing of foliage.

Either top or bottom watering is satisfactory. I like to do both. Bottom watering is easier for routine care. With large spreading plants it takes more time to water carefully from the top, to hit only the soil and let no moisture run down into the crown. It helps to use a long-spouted watering can for top watering. It sneaks under the close foliage, as no pitcher will ever do, but even with this, saucer watering is easier.

However, I am now convinced that some top watering (and there are those who depend on it entirely), is essential to prevent accumulation of fertilizer salts on surface of pot and soil, where they cause stem rot, if petioles touch. Those salts need to be flushed down into the soil. A good way to water from the top is through a little V-shaped opening at the edge of the pot. The V makes a convenient funnel for liquid fertilizing too, which should certainly be done from the top down.

An excellent plan is to give the regular feeding of liquid fertilizing and the next watering from the top. Then you can do quick saucer watering the rest of the time or not, as you wish. When watering from the top, let the *feel* of the soil guide you. It should never be dry, but barely moist at all times. As it tends to dryness, pour enough water on so as to seep out into the saucer. This excess should be emptied after a short time. I now feel sure that plants should not stand in water.

The *amount* of water is determined by the size and type of pot (porous or glazed), the weather (bright or dull, damp or dry), the nature of the soil, even the variety of saintpaulia you are growing. I have long respected the advice of my first African-violet mentor, Elsie Freed: "Give plants as much water in the morning, as will be absorbed by early afternoon. If you give too much, empty the excess by two o'clock. You will soon learn to gauge the right amount."

Wick-fed pots have given many enthusiasts satisfaction and pleasure, and they are decorative. Violet Beauty in a turquoise blue looks very pretty, and White Prince is well set off by yellow. The wicks which are the features of these pots operate on the principle of the oil lamp, with water instead of oil. The containers are of easily cleaned plastic and are wonderfully pretty in pastel shades for a glass window-shelf. They are made in two parts—the upper section is like a flower pot, the lower holds water or liquid fertilizer. From this small reservoir the spun-glass wick draws water through drainage hole into soil. Capillary action draws up water as it is needed. There is little danger of overwatering, and refilling is needed only about every third day. More water should not be added until the full amount is absorbed.

The *quality* of the water must also be considered—hard, soft, or full of chemicals. If you live in the Southwest where water is alkaline or hard, follow the practice of others there and water plants once a month or so with a solution of 1 tablespoon of vinegar to 1 gallon of water. If you have a water softener, draw the water for your plants and let it stand overnight before using. Best of all collect rain water, or melted snow, the natural and most acceptable moisture for all plants, unless it is city rain water, or city snow, when it may be badly contaminated with soot. If you live in the city you may want to rely on distilled water, available at drugstores and filling stations. When water is full of chemicals, you will soon know it from the encrustation which settles on pots, even when no fertilizer has been used. Let such water also stand overnight to free it of gases. Then when you apply it, it will not only be purer, but also of the required room temperature.

CLEANSING OF FOLIAGE

We used to think that a few drops of water on velvety saintpaulia leaves spelled doom. Now we know that nothing is more beneficial than frequent syringing of foliage, provided the water used is of room temperature. Plants collect as much dust as a piano, only you are more likely to see it on a piano than on a dark green leaf, where it is stopping up the breathing pores of the plant. Dusty leaves are no aid to bud development.

If you live in a city area where you can "never keep the house clean," better syringe your violets at least once a week. A rubber sprayer attached to a kitchen faucet that mixes the hot and cold water to the temperature you want is fine, or you can use a misty houseplant syringe or a household insect sprayer from the dime store. Your violets will revel in either treatment. Deal with one plant at a time, hold it on its side under the spray so that the crown will escape soaking. In hot, dry climates frequent syringing is also essential not only to cleanse but to promote humidity. Always let plants dry away from sunshine and out of drafts.

BLESSED HUMIDITY

African violets do not thrive in a hot, dry atmosphere, and assuredly they will not bloom without plenty of humidity. If they do set buds, they will probably drop them unopened, when the atmosphere is too dry. Indeed moist air is another vital key to free flowering. Our violets like to draw in moisture from the air as well as from the soil. In their native habitat, humidity of 60 to 70 percent prevails, so you can see how miserable violets must be in a humidity of 10 to 25 percent, a not-too-uncommon winter condition in some homes and apartments. Although 60 to 70 percent would be dreadful for us, we can maintain areas of 40 to 60 percent and have violets bloom well.

It is worth noting that older violets need less humidity than young ones. Too much for adults results in all sorts of troubles due to fungus, as crown, stem, and leaf rot. Young plants also enjoy the hereditary temperature up to 80 degrees F., possible in covered aquariums.

With most modern heating systems it is difficult to maintain a humid condition. When many plants are grown together humidity is, of course, increased. Pans of water set on radiators or on a table also help by providing a constant source of evaporation. This device is particularly helpful with hot-air systems of heating. There are also electric vaporizers which have been useful under certain conditions. They are hardly suited to a wallpapered living room but in a sunroom could humidify freely.

Many of us have found too that African violets thrive and bloom more freely if each plant is set on a pebble-filled saucer with some water always in it as a ready means of humidifying the surrounding air. Plant pots rest on the stones *above* the constant supply of water in the saucer. Damp sand may be substituted, but I prefer the pebbles.

I have long prized for violets, as well as for other houseplants, zinc trays (but copper is nicer), made by a plumber to fit broad window sills. The trays are an inch deep and spread with white roofing pebbles, the same as narcissus bulbs are grown in. The trays hold a quantity of water. The drip from top watering runs in, and I pour a lot more directly into the tray. Pots rest on the pebbles, *above* the level of water, which, evaporating, creates a healthful aura of humidity. This makes me extremely popular with my saintpaulias, if their blooming is any indication of affection.

If you don't want the bother of getting a special tray, you can use one of the ready-made, metal window boxes, filling it with pebbles or sand to the proper level. Chick feeders, the type sold at poultry supply houses for half-grown chicks, also have possibilities. You can buy them in lengths to suit your window, but you must solder the joints to make them waterproof and paint the inside with an asphalt paint. Remove the wire guards, then fill with sand. Keep this moist, not puddled, and set your violets on top. The additional humidity from the wet sand will please them no end.

In a terrarium, aquarium, or battery jar, with a pane of glass placed over the opening, most pleasant and humid conditions can be constantly maintained, but it is important to keep such plantings out of the sun or they will be far too hot. It is also necessary each day to raise the glass at the top and air the plants for a few minutes. Very attractive groups can be arranged for such glassed-in plantings. Particularly charming are purple African violets, pink wax begonias (provided they carry no mite), and delicate maidenhair ferns, which are likewise dependent on humidity. Only if these glass gardens are kept too wet will there be signs of decay. With so little moisture escaping, almost no watering is required. Bubble bowls, such as hold berried Christmas arrangements, are also nice for group plantings, and hardly need a glass cover. Use young rather than old plants, however, in these arrangements since the very high humidity may be too much for mature violets.

PURPOSE OF SOIL

When it comes to a soil mixture, it's better to get a grasp of the principles involved, than to follow blindly formulas laid down by others, no matter how handsome their violets may be. Any formula must start with the soil in the place where you live, and that differs in Massachusetts and Virginia from what it is in, say, California or Iowa.

The purpose of soil is twofold—to support roots, and to offer an adequate food supply. Soil should be of such a consistency that roots can easily penetrate, and open enough to be well aerated, that is not so heavy or sticky when wet as to be impervious to air. Some enthusiasts grow plants in vermiculite alone, but only count on it to support roots. For food, they give regular applications of liquefied fertilizer. Others grow violets satisfactorily without soil, in water supplied with a nourishing chemical formula. For support, wire-basket devices are employed. Some of us use small pots, some large ones. The users of small containers consider soil mostly for support. They feed their plants about twice as much as those whose violets grow in larger pots, already containing an adequate amount of well-balanced, fertile soil.

Many of us have been interested in Mr. H. G. Harvey's weekly 1-2-3-4 formula for a sequence of weekly treatments—B 1 solution (manufacturer's minimum dosage); superphosphate, ¼ teaspoon to 1 quart of water; B 1 again; Hyponex, ¼ teaspoon to 1 quart of water; all repeated, month after month. But how many who followed Mr. Harvey's excellent regime for his own plants noted that they were in "a relatively deficient soil, ⅓ woods dirt and ¹⁄₅₀ of the total volume of sheep manure being the only elements in the soil that fed the plants?"

If you followed this schedule, your plants may have lacked nitrogen which Mr. Harvey's already had, or they may have had too much of phosphates and potash, because these were already present in your soil. The B 1, of course, is a conditioner, not a food. It releases needed elements, which, without its action, may be present but not available to plants.

Almost all violets will do well on the old equal-thirds formula of garden loam, leafmold or peatmoss, and sand. This mixture is light enough to be easily penetrated by the fine root system of saintpaulias, open enough to receive air, spongy enough because of the leafmold or peatmoss, to retain moisture long enough, but not too long; the garden loam offers varying degrees of nourishment. If it is good enough for potatoes, it's balanced enough for saintpaulias.

If you have only a few pots of violets, or are quite inexperienced, you may not want to bother concocting a special soil. There are excellent packaged mixtures now available from reputable and successful growers. And these mixtures are already sterilized. If you are making up equal thirds, (soil, sand, and leafmold), the mixture must be sterilized (see page 125) to avoid nematode infection.

ABOUT FERTILIZERS

Because you are after superior not average results, you will probably decide to supplement the equal thirds with liquid feedings of one of the concentrated commercial plant foods. Weekly feedings of Hyponex—¼ teaspoon to 1 quart of water—have brought success to many collectors, and this dose is given all the plants, seedlings and mature specimens, regardless of size. Although this dosage is not exactly in line with the manufacturer's directions, it certainly has the endorsement of Old Man Experience, whom we can all respect. However, I don't believe in depending on just one brand of plant food, even if each is "complete." Balance of elements varies. Proliferol, Roigina, Afri-Gro, Spoonit, Liqua-vita, Plant-Tabs, and Virdans Plant Tonic are all possibilities. It is wise to alternate commercial products, and also to use Vitamin B 1 in solution, perhaps once a month, to make sure that all food elements are being released. At our present state of knowledge, the use of even old manure would seem questionable. It is a possible carrier for certain pests and diseases, and if it is sterilized in the soil mixture, its most valuable element, nitrogen, is almost all lost.

In discussing or buying fertilizers, a number of terms are used which are not always entirely familiar to beginners.

Organic fertilizers are those composed of once-living matter, as animal manure, blood, bone meal, hoof and horn meal; or vegetable residues—grass, leaves, stems, hay, cottonseed meal; or *natural* mineral products, as ground limestone, phosphate rock, etc.

Inorganic fertilizers are chemical products, artificially manufactured—nitrate of soda, ammonium sulphate, and muriate of potash.

Commercial fertilizers are packaged or bagged products usually containing both organic and inorganic materials with, if they are good, a fair amount of organic matter and often this quantity indicated, as "40 percent of the nitrogen from organic sources." Many carry labeled percentages of the most vital elements. For instance a 15-30-15 means 15 percent of nitrogen, 30 percent of phosphorus, and 15 percent of potash. The remaining 40 percent is some inert carrier with no fertility value.

Nitrogen promotes leaf and stem strength and stimulates growth generally. Too much makes plants spindly and poor at flower production, and inclined to bud drop. You can obtain one source, ammonium sulphate, at the drugstore. Use 1 tablespoon to 1 gallon of water. It may improve a stunted or yellowed condition in one week.

Phosphorus is for roots. It also gives a steady push to flower and seed production. Too little results in poor foliage color. Too much makes growth sappy, lacking in fiber, and weak so that the whole plant has a floppy look. Bone meal is a good source. Allow 1 teaspoon to 1 four-inch pan of soil.

Potash is the antitoxin among plant foods. It wards off disease, stabilizes growth, and intensifies color. Lacking it, a plant has a dull look; flowers have no luster. Wood ashes are one source. Their strength varies with different woods. A 5-inch potful to 1 bushel of soil is safe.

"Trace elements"—iron, boron, manganese—in small amounts are also necessary to healthy plant life.

Ailing plants should not be fed, unless you have every reason to believe they are starving. Usually sick plants are suffering from almost anything except lack of food. Check on the program of Brief Guidance at the end of this chapter, before you start feeding a plant that looks under par. Maybe humidity or light or watering is at fault.

It is also a good idea to withhold food for a week or so after a big bout of blooming. Most plants have peaks and valleys of flowering. They require a little peace and quiet after production in order to gather their resources again. They should not be urged too quickly from their rest. This is certainly true of the large-flowered varieties. Doubles being naturally very floriferous seem to need less rest, more food, and more water than the singles.

THE ACIDITY PROBLEM

As for acidity, the last word as to saintpaulia preference is certainly yet to be said. It may well be we will finally conclude that the saintpaulia is one of those plants of amenable disposition which grows well in neutral, or slightly sweet, or slightly acid mediums—pH6.8 to pH7.2 (pH7 being neutral). Degree of acidity certainly influences color of flower and foliage, even if the margin one way or another is still within the realm of health. Acidity brings out redness in leaves and deepens the blueness of blossoms. We see it obviously in hydrangeas, which turn from pink to blue when moved from sweet to sour or acid soil.

You can check on soil acidity with a home-testing kit sold at hardware or garden-supply stores. Too much acidity can be corrected by mixing ground limestone in with the soil to sweeten it. If the soil is too sweet, and responsible for rather pallid flowers and very light green leaves, use an acid leafmold for the humus. That from under an old oak tree or beneath pine trees, where needles are really decomposed, may turn the trick.

The sure way to proceed is to have soil from the area you intend for potting, analyzed. This is a free service available to state residents. (See page 91ff.) Ask for a *complete* analysis. You may as well get the whole story, not just a sweet-sour comment.

WATER CULTURE IN VASES

One easy way to get quantity and size of bloom—a riot from Blue Boy and Blue Girl and two-inch flowers almost all the time on Pink Beauty—is to grow some plants the decorative way in goblets or vases of water. In winter, when cut flowers are expensive, you can have blossoms for every room by growing violets in this way. For a dinner party, make a lovely centerpiece by placing individual plants in jelly glasses or custard cups and grouping them in a low bowl, perhaps with pieces of ivy or philodendron inserted to give the design line, as the flower arrangers say. I always keep rooted pieces of vines in water in winter for this purpose.

The water culture method for violets is simple enough. Select containers of a size to support crowns well above the level of the water and preferably of colored glass or pottery. Rooting seems stronger in these opaque vessels than in clear ones. Fill them, but three-quarters full, with distilled water, fortified with Hyponex, Proliferol, or whatever plant food you use for your earth-bound saintpaulias, and at the same strength, as ¼ teaspoon perhaps to 1 quart distilled water. By all means add two or three pieces of charcoal to insure sweetness of the water for a long period.

As evaporation takes place, add more of the solution. After three or four weeks, start over again. Throw out the accumulation, wash vases in hot water, and set the violets in fresh solution. If sometimes lower leaves look gray or feel a little soft, put the plants back on plain water for a week or two. Afterwards take care to keep the water level lower. Perhaps you have exceeded the three-quarter recommendation and your plants are waterlogged. You can easily avoid this and have all kinds of artistic arrangements the water way. And in case you wish to describe this beautiful method impressively to a friend you could say, "It's done with hydroponics."

POT SIZES

As for pots, I believe now that bloom is promoted by the "tight shoe," although very handsome leafy specimens develop in somewhat oversized azalea or bulb pans, as the low, broad flower pots are called. However, no matter how handsome the leaves, how interesting their pattern, or lovely their color, the cry always is—WE WANT BLOOM!

Just how cramped you will keep your plants to achieve this depends on the space you have for them and the fertilizing program you prefer. So long as the outside of the ball of earth shows a covering of fine white roots (no brown ones, please) you should get flowers, if general culture is good. The earth ball should not look like a ball of white string. When it is heavily covered with roots, it's time for a shift, unless you are a devotee of the small-pot-and-heavy-feeding program with small jardinieres or other decorative containers perhaps to support a wide spread of leaves. It rather depends on how plants look best to you. Personally a great spreading specimen in a tiny pot always reminds me of a fat lady in tight shoes. The whole set up makes me nervous. I like a balanced look, and I prefer bulb pans to pots. I admire the plant form of the saintpaulia and feel it develops to beautiful advantage only when it has room to spread.

In any case don't overpot. Don't be *at* it all the time. Put your half-inch seedlings and your rooted leaves into 2-inch pots right off, and let the youngsters stay there about a year. Then shift to 3-inch pots or 4-inch bulb pans, and again let your plants alone. Such quarters will be adequate for a long time, if the soil you are using is well balanced and you give extra plant food as well as fertilizer. (Of course, sick plants need to be depotted and examined. If something upsets drainage, you have to repot to set things straight again.)

This is general advice which *you* must interpret. Some of the heftiest growers like the duPont varieties and those of the Supreme strain only come into full beauty in 5's or 6's, but let them reach that great estate gradually, on a yearly basis, as growth indicates need. When they have an 8- or 9-inch leaf spread, they are ready. Too often people think that repotting is a panacea. They look at an ailing plant and decide right off it needs a bigger pot, or for that matter they look at a healthy one and just feel like doing something to it, so they repot.

If a plant is ailing, it probably needs less room. Roots may be rotted and the whole system need cutting back and repotting in a smaller, not a larger, pot.

SINGLE OR MULTIPLE CROWNS

Your attitude toward size of container must also be influenced by *your* preference for single or multiple-crowned plants. Please don't let anyone tell you which you should prefer. If you like them bunchy, have them so. There are those who say that "every time you have to divide a plant because it has developed a multiple crown, you admit poor care of the plant—to let the multiple crown develop," but I don't agree. It's a matter of taste. A large multiple-crowned plant, shifted on to a 5- or 6-inch bulb pan so that it has adequate root room, can be very handsome and decorative.

Show schedules generally require that exhibition plants be

single crowned, and they give real point value to a whorl of evenly spaced leaves. If you are exhibiting or prefer "single crowners," keep a watch out for suckers. Snip them off with tweezers while they are tiny and their removal will not leave a scar. Be sure though you aren't snipping off buds. They sometimes first appear with leaves on each side of what is to be the flower stem. If you aren't sure, wait and see development before reaching for the tweezers.

Considerable suckering may be a symptom of trouble. Crowded roots or lack of light may lead to thick bunchy growth. There may also be heavy suckering with mite infestation, a sort of desperate effort for survival. Any neglect of vital needs is likely to result in suckering, though suckering is not necessarily caused by neglect.

When you get plants from an African violet specialist, they will usually be in 2-, 2¼-, or 3-inch pots. Since growers try to have budding plants for their customers many, not all, of the violets you buy will be ready to shift on to 3's or 4's, so it's a good idea to have some larger pots or pans ready. Also have some sterilized soil at hand.

If you receive gift plants which have been supplied by a commercial florist, these will usually be multiple-crowned and in 3's or 4's, particularly if the variety is White Lady. Examination may reveal a potbound condition. If so, and only if so, shift your plant on, as it is, to a 4-inch pot or pan, or you can separate the multiple crown into sections. Pull, don't cut apart, and when a growing unit clings stubbornly and separation will involve cutting, better leave the group as one. Too often cut plants are lost plants. If in pulling, you tear, brush over damaged areas with Fermate or dusting sulphur. Either will promote healthy healing and deter fungous trouble.

Several sections may be well spaced in the larger pot or pan, or the singles may be set individually in as small pots as possible, probably 2's. If you break off any leaves in the potting process, remember each is a potential plant. Keep divided plants somewhat "on the dry side" and out of full sun till new growth indicates the divisions have taken hold. If you have little room for a collection and pine for numerous varieties, you had better put shifting and big plants out of your mind. Stick to 2's or 2¼'s, water frequently (usually daily except in dull weather), and feed weekly. One window fitted with glass shelves will hold a lot of 2's, and then of course there is always the top of your husband's desk or his bureau for the big ones you can't bear to part with!

ART OF POTTING

Use only the cleanest of pots—either new ones (soaked for hours so that they won't draw untold amounts of moisture from the soil), or old ones, sterilized with a thorough dousing in boiling water. One little crumb of old soil can carry nematodes to a whole collection, so play safe when you use a pot that has held another plant. Water each plant well a few hours before moving it so the soil will be firm, neither soggy nor crumbly.

To depot a plant, slide your left hand over the top of the pot with the plant crown between your first and second fingers, grasping the rim of the pot lightly. With your right hand, turn it upside down, over your left, knock against a table or with a pencil push through the drainage hole to ease the plant out of the pot. Soil should stay all in one piece, without any breakage of roots. Even the bit of crocking (piece of flower pot), should still be in the place it occupied above the drainage hole.

To shift on a healthy plant, select for it a pot one full size larger, that is one more inch across the top, but no more. Fit an arching piece of flower pot over the drainage hole. Then put in half an inch, or proportionately more for large pots, of coarse soil, that is with twiggy stony bits in it, or use a layer of charcoal or small stones. Such roughage facilitates drainage in 3-inch or larger pots. Plants in smaller pots need only one piece of crocking.

Next start filling in the soil mixture. Try the plant now for size. Is there too much or too little soil underneath it? Don't set it too high. At the top you want half an inch space left from crown to rim surface. You want more for larger plants. If you are transplanting an older specimen with a somewhat denuded crown, perhaps a plant which is recovering from something, set it rather low in the pot so as to cover up the disaster area.

As you fill in soil, firm it well with an inch-wide stick; a ruler or piece of lath makes a fine "potting stick." Let's have no air pockets. Plant your plants, don't float them. Tap the bottom of the pot on a firm surface to settle soil for sure around the roots. Firm the center—and the plant should be centered—with your thumbs, and finally do a finished job with a little sifted soil on the surface, not higher however than the necessary half inch.

If removal of pot reveals a decayed root area or your plant is suffering from crown rot, cut sharply away everything soft. Leave no speck of brown to corrupt the rest. With your fingers

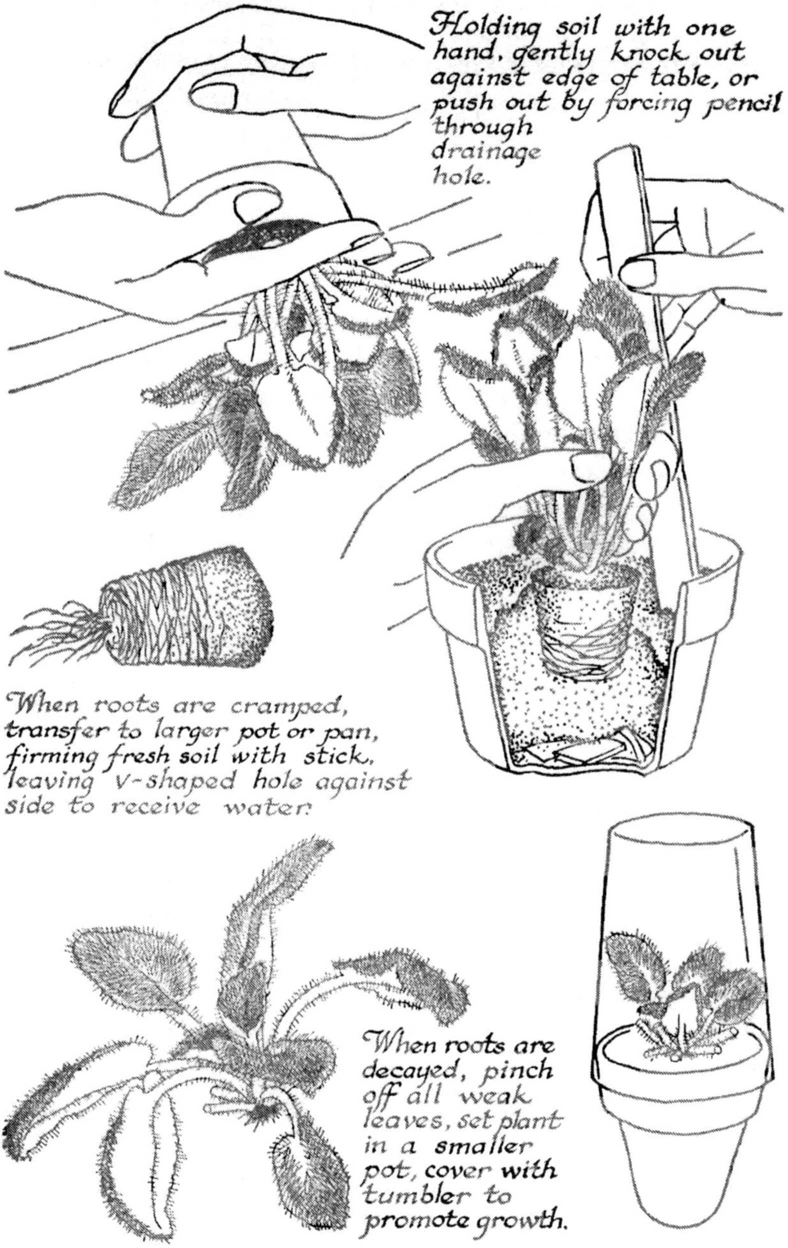
Holding soil with one hand, gently knock out against edge of table, or push out by forcing pencil through drainage hole.
When roots are cramped, transfer to larger pot or pan, firming fresh soil with stick, leaving V-shaped hole against side to receive water.
When roots are decayed, pinch off all weak leaves, set plant in a smaller pot, cover with tumbler to promote growth.

How to Repot a Plant

work away as much old soil as possible. You may not have much plant left, since you will have to remove some of the larger leaves, if you reduce the root system considerably. There must be a healthy balance. You can't safely prune the bottom and not prune the top. A dusting with sulphur or Fermate will keep the cut areas from rotting, and a light covering with a stimulant like Rootone will encourage growth. Repot such a reduced plant in the smallest possible pot it will take and place a glass or small jar over the top to give it a "greenhouse" while it recovers.

Shifted plants, as opposed to repotted ones, should experience no shock. They are just moving along to roomier quarters. Repotted plants were already in poor condition or they wouldn't require so much disturbance. They will come back slowly, but chances are they *will* come back.

SUMMER HOLIDAY

All houseplants thrive on an outdoor summer. It's like camping for city children. Every element lacking or contrived in their indoor life, nature bountifully provides outside—humidity and fresh air particularly.

But with our violets, certain precautions must be taken, if they are to have good looks as well as good health in the fall, and be ready to bloom freely again indoors. Their brittle foliage requires protection from winds and the mud splatter incidental to heavy rain. They need shade and, of course, they must not be depotted and set directly in the ground. This would necessitate cutting stray roots to fit pots again in the fall and result in September convalescence instead of September health.

Almost every small property will have an ideal spot for saintpaulias in summer, perhaps under an arching shrub or thick-leaved tree. Either will give protection from strong sunshine, wind, and occasional hail.

The shade of a building which also cuts off wind is another possibility. I have a little ell between house and garage where African violets can be "planted" among true violets, whose leaves spread nicely over the soil in the pots. Alma Wright has found her violets liked to summer under the barn shed. Perhaps there is a shaded pool on your place where violets may grow through the summer in lovely association with lacy ferns and other woodsy plant life. If pachysandra or myrtle grows under a tree as ground cover—and is not yet impenetrable—sink the pots among these plants, and if it's myrtle, draw the foliage across the soil to avoid splatter.

For sure protection from mud, cover the soil in the pots with a mulch of peatmoss or stone chips, as deep as you can arrange it under every violet's leaf spread. To deter tunneling worms spread ashes or cinders under each pot as you sink it. If you are preparing a whole bed for the sinkage, make a layer three inches deep before placing the pots and filling soil in around them.

Wherever they go outdoors, remember saintpaulias are not desert plants. Inevitably they will need watering in addition to rainfall, which can be very unreliable some summers. So plant within reach of the hose, and enlist a neighbor's help if you go on vacation. Nature alone in these parts is not entirely trustworthy when it comes to watering potted plants. Their restricted roots cannot forage for moisture in the manner of a peony or a forsythia.

Perhaps you will have some expendable violets from seed sown in the spring. Why not treat these as annuals? Plant a lovely bed of them for summer pleasure. Even after light frost, they will give a little bloom.

Porch summers are also pleasing to violets. Set them out of strong sunshine and wind, and they will bloom freely and decoratively, and be thoroughly refreshed come fall. I use a white, Victorian, wire step stand on the porch where violets look charming with the indoor philodendron vines. Failing outdoor possibilities, you can give your violets healthful days by keeping the windows open as much as possible, and syringing tops often in very hot weather.

If you live in California, you can provide a lathhouse for your violets. So long as night temperatures do not go much below 60 degrees F., they will be safe—and look lovely with fuchsias perhaps and ferns. The lath must be placed close enough to ward off noonday sun, and through the rainless summer, considerable syringing under the benches will be necessary to increase humidity. These lathhouses, possible in California, are the envy of every visiting gardener from the East. Going into the small flowery "rooms" is like entering a corner of the Garden of Eden.

BRIEF GUIDANCE TO BLOOM

1. *Light.* Give all possible light and as much sun as foliage will stand without bleaching. Any window is right, if strong sunlight is filtered by a thin curtain. Try "shocking" non-bloomers into flower with strong sunshine.

2. *Turn plants* a little each week so that all growing parts

TO MAKE THEM BLOOM

will receive about the some amount of light. Then development will be uniform.

3. *Temperature.* For daytime, try for 70 to 72 degrees F.; at night a drop of about 10 degrees is healthful.

4. *Ventilation.* Admit fresh air once or twice daily, but *indirectly* in cold weather. Not a breath of escaping gas, please!

5. *Watering.* Room-temperature water is required. It can usually be applied from top or bottom, but must be from the top after a fertilizing, and often enough from the top at other times to keep fertilizing salts from collecting on the soil surface.

6. *Cleansing of Foliage.* Spray with room-temperature water often enough to keep tops clean. Frequency depends on locality. Once a week is usually fine. Dry plants away from sun and drafts.

7. *Humidity.* Bloom depends on enough of it. Increase average living-room amount with pans or vases of water set on or near radiators as a source of evaporation, by grouping plants, by special devices of pebble- or sand-filled saucers and trays, or with a humidifier.

8. *Soil.* A mixture of equal thirds of garden loam, leafmold or peatmoss, and sand is fine. Be fancier if you want to.

9. *Fertilizer.* Give all plants, young and old, light, weekly feedings of your favorite liquefied plant food.

10. *Pot Size.* Use as small pots as plants will take without developing a matted earth ball. The "tight shoe" promotes bloom.

11. *Soil Sterilizing.* Bake all soil for 1 hour at 180 degrees F. or fumigate with a commercial preparation to prevent nematode attacks on roots. (See page 125ff.)

12. *Spraying.* Pick your pest deterrent, and spray regularly,

usually once a month. Guard healthy plants; then you won't have to nurse sick ones, or figure out ailments, and what to do about them. (See Chapter Six.)

13. *"Free Gifts."* Mistrust all strangers, all gift plants, all boarders. Isolate newcomers for 2 months before introducing them to your treasured collection. You can spot mite trouble in that time, and, if necessary, discard the one plant. Your collection will not have been contaminated.

14. *Summer Quarters.* Holidays outside promote health and bloom. Place out of wind and in shade. Mulch to avoid mud splatter. Plunge in the ground, set on the porch, or keep house windows near plants open most of the time.

15. *Your First Eight.* Make haste slowly. Enjoy while you learn. Start with easy, inexpensive varieties in a fine range of color (whites and pinks are the hardest to make bloom well). Try: Bicolor, Blue No. 32, Mentor Boy, Norseman, Orchid Girl (Red Head Girl), Pink Beauty, Red King, Snow Prince.

CHAPTER TWO

New Plants from Old

His leaf also shall not wither; and whatsoever he doeth shall prosper.
PSALM I, 3

Is there such a thing as one saintpaulia, just one? I doubt it. I have never known anybody to be satisfied with a single plant. Even if a present is received from a florist, it is usually obvious, even to an inexperienced eye, that the pot holds possibilities of more than one plant. So first it's a matter of separating and re-potting. Then the "secret of the leaf" is learned, and from then on, no limits are in sight. Indeed, no, there can never be just one saintpaulia.

Probably no other plant offers four easier possibilities of increase. (1) You can divide plants with a multiple crown. (2) You can start new plants from suckers. (3) You can root leaves in earth or water. These are all "vegetative" methods involving green parts of the plant. You can also (4) grow a tremendous crop from one packet or one podful of seed, as I will disclose in the chapters which follow.

NEW PLANTS BY DIVISION

If you have a plant with more than one crown, you can *with care* separate it into a number of smaller individual plants. Let it dry out a little before the operation. Dry soil and dry roots are easier to cope with than wet ones. Also, dry roots can be more readily pulled apart. First remove the pot. Then spread the plant out on a newspaper and very gently but firmly pull the sections apart. Without any trouble at all you will get two or three simple divisions.

The rest, a clump of two or three crowns, will probably cling stubbornly together. You can pot the whole thing and grow on a nice plant with a multiple crown, or take a chance, not always successful, and with a sharp knife cut it into single crowns. If you do any cutting, rub the parts with sulphur, or half-and-half Fermate and talc, so as to discourage unfriendly fungous organisms. Then grow all the divisions on the dry side, even letting them go to the point of slight wilting. Cuts will heal faster that way, and recovery be more likely.

Two-inch-diameter pots or the smallest-sized pan will not be too large for divisions with some root system. With plenty of surface room, plants soon develop their large handsome leaves to the fullest and maintain an open crown from which an almost constant procession of flowering stems will push forth. Use the same soil as before—equal thirds of sand, loam, and leafmold or humus—or use leafmold alone, if that is easier for you. Be sure the mixture has been sterilized. (See page 125ff.)

Suckers growing out at the sides of the crown are another source of new plants. Let them get big enough to get hold of—

and distinguish between them and an oncoming flower—before you cut them sharply away. Rub the cuts on parent and offspring with sulphur, or Fermate, and on the sucker, use a very light dusting of Rootone or Proliferol powder to stimulate root growth. Then plant each sucker in a 2-inch pot, and grow it also a little on the dry side to discourage rot.

"PUT DOWN A LEAF"

It is no trick at all to grow new plants from leaves. Select firm, medium-sized ones, preferably not from the last most mature "ring" of old leaves. (However, almost any leaf or part of a leaf will grow, and some even swear by the tiniest ones, which are more difficult to handle.) If a "violet friend" mails you a leaf and it looks wilted on arrival, soak the whole thing overnight before you start it on its way.

Cut leaves with long petioles (stems) from the parent plant. These, rooted in water or in a sandy soil mixture or in vermiculite, develop into flowering-sized plants in about eight to nine months, rarely in six, but the length of time depends on cultural conditions and also on the nature of the variety being propagated. Sometimes within a year, leaf-grown plants are large enough for division. So all you really need to satisfy even an unlimited enthusiasm for African violets is a few leaves from plants of the varieties you admire and, of course, considerable patience.

Many persons are using vermiculite, a mica product which comes by the bag and has the advantage of being already sterilized. The coarser particles are fine to include in the potting mixture, the finer part for rooting leaves, and the finest for planting seeds. If vermiculite is pressed through a quarter-inch mesh screen, it readily separates into material of different degrees of coarseness. Most of those who have used this medium consider it a preventative of crown rot, and find that it aids the development of the plant. If you start leaves in vermiculite, try watering them every 10 days with a *weak* solution of a good plant food like Hyponex, Liqua-vita, or Proliferol, Spoonit, or your own favorite. Any of these will supply the slight first nourishment required.

ROOTING LEAVES IN WATER

Here are two practical methods developed for leaf propagation by home gardeners. Cover a water-filled glass tumbler with wax paper held in place with a rubber band. Pierce the paper in 3 places. Insert 3 leaf stems in these holes and deeply enough for the stems to reach into the water. Set the glass in a fully light but not sunny window. If you use faucet rather than rain water, let it stand uncovered for 24 hours beforehand so that all chlorine may be released. Or you can use distilled water, which can be purchased from a drugstore or filling station.

It is also possible to work even more simply. In a shallow glass dish or soup bowl a number of different varieties can easily be started. Just fill the dish with enough small stones to support the leaf stems, and maintain a sufficient supply of water to keep the ends of the stems moist. If you have it, tuck bits of charcoal among the stones to keep the water sweet.

In 2 to 4 weeks, depending on variety and location, roots will appear. Change the water then unless you have used charcoal. By the end of another week or so a small green leaf may appear at the base of each parent leaf. If the parent leaf has begun to deteriorate, transfer the rooted leaves to a 2- or 3-inch pot of light soil or pure sand. If the parent leaf remains firm and healthy, wait until an inch-long cluster of leaves appears. Make the transfer from water to soil with all possible care, spooning the plantlet from aquatic to terrestrial life, and spreading the roots out gently in the soil mixture.

The time for rooting varies. Ionantha leaves root very quickly, I notice, while the duPont varieties certainly take their time. No leaves can be depended upon to produce roots very promptly, but so long as the parent leaf remains healthy and does not soften and decay, the growth of roots and new leaves will eventually occur. Sometimes it actually takes months. The amount of growth also varies. The heavier growers—duPonts, Ruffles, and the Amazon and Supreme strains—send up fewer growth clusters (as they do flowers), than Blue Boys and Neptunes, which can be counted on for six or seven.

When quite a group of new leaves appears, cut the parent leaf away. Remove it sooner if it shows signs of deterioration, but often it is not necessary to discard it for a long time. If a variety is scarce or your supply limited, you may be able to grow a second or even a third crop of saintpaulias from the same treasured leaf. Each time you will, of course, be working with a shorter, sharply cut petiole until a third planting is made perhaps with no petiole at all and only the leaf base to insert in the soil. Even so, you can expect success, as many have found from experience that the same leaf will produce as fine a third crop

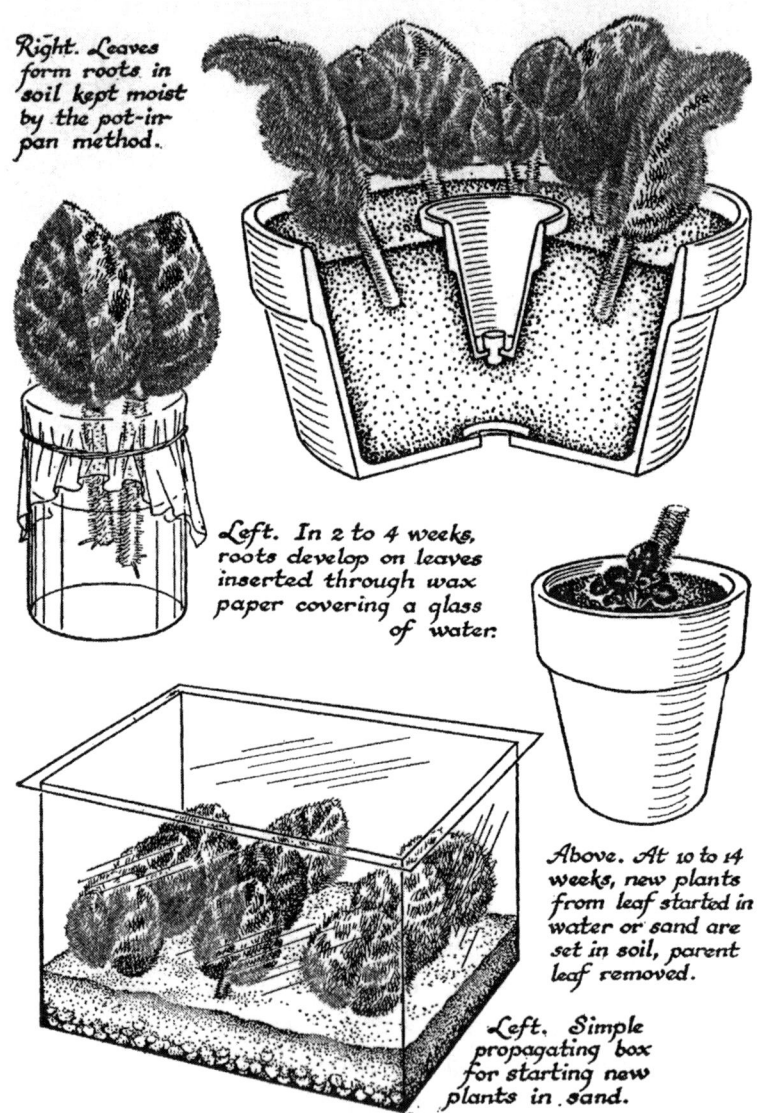

Methods of Propagation with Leaves

Methods of Propagation with Leaves

as it did a first. This is particularly true of duPont Lavender Pink which being a slow and valuable grower is always cherished down to the last leaf.

Expect some little setback at the time of the water-to-soil transfer while roots are adjusting to the new medium. In less than 5 months, however, you will have a well-established, thrifty plant which should, in less than a year, produce flowers.

As you grow in knowledge, you may want to experiment by starting plants from leaves without stems. The Browns of Newman, Georgia, say it makes a difference. I don't know. It would probably take a great deal of experiment to prove their theory. They say, "If we are trying to perpetuate a *flower* sport, we propagate the full leaf without removing any of the petiole. If we are trying to perpetuate a *leaf* change, we remove the petiole even into the leaf . . . Our theory is that the point of inception of a leaf change is in the leaf, not in the stem, and that the inception of a bloom change is in the trunk of the plant."

ROOTING LEAVES IN SOIL

A second method has been developed by enthusiasts who prefer to start their plants in soil, or a soil substitute like vermiculite. They have found that battery jars, terrariums, and aquariums are excellent makeshift greenhouses for propagating, or even a pot or deep ash tray with a drinking glass inverted over it.

Over the bottom of a fish bowl or other suitable receptacle spread an inch of pebbles. Cover the small stones with a couple of inches of fine, sterilized, sandy soil, moist but not made soggy. Then insert the violet leaves just deeply enough for them to escape the soil surface. If they rest on it, decay may start. (If you have trouble making the leaves stand up, prop them with toothpicks or hairpins.) However, in experiments at the Missouri Botanical Garden, two plants of Blue Boy out of many hundreds, showed viviparous characteristics with "plantlets developing directly on the leaf blade," when the base of the leaf and not the end of the petiole was in direct contact with the growing medium. Amateurs have also reported this tendency.

Firm the soil mixture or vermiculite well around each stem. Set the makeshift greenhouse in a light but not sunny place. If it has no top, stretch a kitchen-bowl cover over it or a piece of cellophane secured by a rubber band.

Little attention will now be needed for several weeks. The first few days after you plant, inspect the soil to be sure you moistened it well enough at the start for it to stay damp. If moisture collects on the sides of the glass, remove the cover long enough to wipe away the excess. In a not too warm and not sunny place such attention will hardly be necessary. In 4 to 6 weeks the rooted leaves will be at the new-plant stage, and ready for separate potting. Some who have followed this plan report bloom on new plants in 6 months.

POT-IN-PAN METHOD

Then there is the pot-in-pan method. Use moist, sterilized sand, or sand and peatmoss, or vermiculite for a rooting medium. Fill a large porous bulb pan with this and into the center insert a small stoppered flowerpot. Keep the small center pot filled with water. The amount of water will decrease because of slow seepage through the walls of the inner pot. This seepage provides the surrounding soil area with adequate and even moisture. Insert the leaf stems in the soil at a slight angle, the upper surfaces to the front. In 2 to 4 weeks roots will form, and in the course of another month, new sprouts will push up to the surface. In 3 months' time, well-developed plants will be ready for separate potting.

The value of root stimulants for saintpaulias is not entirely clear yet. There are both pro and con reports of their effect on speed of rooting. Generally it is felt that Rootone and Proliferol, if they do not make development quicker, do make it better, and that *lightly* dipped cuttings produce stronger, larger root systems.

In any case, rooting and flowering seem to be hastened by a spring rather than an autumn start. There are a few reports of late September flowering from early May propagating. Perhaps the old idea that leaf-to-blossom took a year was based on autumn and winter propagating. Even so, flowering in less than 8 months is fairly unusual.

Any one of these methods—glass of water, aquarium or other makeshift greenhouse, pot-in-pan, or your own variation of them—will start a violet collection for you or increase the valued number already in hand.

PROBLEMS OF VARIEGATION

Why African violets develop variegated leaves and how to propagate variegations remain a major mystery. Like other saintpaulia matters, we shall doubtless have more light on all this before long, since the subject has the attention of both scientists

Variegated Type, DuPont Lavender Pink

and amateurs. Evidently the condition we see and refer to as variegation is of two kinds, one caused by certain environmental conditions, as soil deficiency or even pot binding, the other, as in Blue Girl, a true variegation that can be inherited.

When the colored areas on a leaf run into each other and are not sharply defined, plants are usually suffering from a soil deficiency, probably absence of iron or manganese or other trace elements essential to the production of chlorophyll. Streaking in particular may indicate manganese deficiency. Restore balance to the soil and the "variegated" leaves may die or lose their variegation. It is even possible to starve or pot bind a plant into greater variegation. Propagate leaves from such variegateds and all may be green, unless you supply the rooting leaves with the same deficiencies of soil as those of the parent plant.

White or albino plants are examples of an almost complete absence of chlorophyll. Usually their life is brief, for they represent an atrophied condition. Leaves from albinos rarely root. If they do, the subsequent crop is green.

True variegation is a mutation. As such it can be transmitted to its seedlings, but since variegation seems to be a recessive characteristic, few plants will reveal it, and perhaps none in the first generation. Although it is said that some variegated plants were observed in the first plantings found in Africa, there were not many, and acres of greenhouse plants today may include few that come variegated.

The Tinari's say that normally they wouldn't expect more than one variegated out of 5000 plants. But one spring they put to root a row of S. ionantha—50 to 75 leaf cuttings—and the plantlets on all these cuttings, every one, were variegated. That same spring they noticed considerable variegation elsewhere in the greenhouses. The next spring there weren't six variegateds in all, a slight percentage. They suspect that certain weather conditions, temperatures etc. are conducive to variegation.

In true variegation, as distinguished from bleaching or chlorosis, the colored areas are sharply defined and not irregularly merging. Even under the most favorable cultural conditions, true variegation remains. It is not dependent on a soil lack. According to Orland E. White of the University of Virginia, the type, of which Blue Girl is an example, "appears to involve the different kinds of tissues, one chlorophyll defective, and the other normal green . . . It is a chimaera phenomenon (a mixture of tissues of different genetic constitution in the same part of a plant.)"

The surest way to propagate variegation is to divide a plant or to take suckers from it. The plantlets that grow from the base of a petiole as in leaf propagation, form from the soft inner tissue, or cambium—and it seems very possible, according to H. M. Butterfield of the University of California, that variegation is "limited to the surface tissue, rather than extending into the cambium."

Alma Wright notices an increasing number of variegated plants in private collections, and these are known to have produced variegated offspring regularly. She has such a plant, a White Lady, the cuttings of which produce mingled cream and green foliage. She feels that in some mysterious way, variegation can become fixed in a particular individual *plant* rather than in a variety, and that plants of white varieties are possibly more likely to show this tendency than varieties of other colors.

BRIEF GUIDANCE TO MORE PLANTS

1. *Divisions.* Separate plants with more than one crown or center of growth. Remove pot, gently pull apart, and plant divisions separately in as small pots as possible. Cut tight sections apart at your own risk. Rub cuts with sulphur or Fermate. Grow on the dry side at first.

2. *Suckers or side growths.* Cut off and pot separately in two-inch pots. Rub cuts with sulphur or Fermate.

3. *Leaves.* Break off with long stems. Root in water, vermiculite, sand, or a light soil mixture. See illustration, *Methods of Propagation with Leaves,* pages 52 and 53. (Plants on exhibit are really *not* proper sources for your private supply of leaves. We must all try to promote a more honorable attitude toward show plants. Too often these come home just about picked clean of foliage. It's really only fair to respect people's plants as we do their pocketbooks, and other private possessions.)

CHAPTER THREE

Planned Parenthood

A mighty maze, but not without a plan.
ALEXANDER POPE

Some folks like to start at the beginning. For them growing plants from seed is the *only* way—and preferably from seed of their own pollinating. Otherwise they feel they see the show only after Act I is over.

Of course, there is one trouble in letting everybody know what fun it is to cross their own saintpaulias. They are bound to raise many "new" varieties, and if considerable judgment is not used, there will be no end to these ever-increasing name lists, which to me at least are positively alarming. With all this seeding going on we must be more critical of new varieties, more willing to be rid of old ones, if they have been surpassed.

It may be true "there is no child like my child," but we must develop saintpaulia self-control. Evidently Alma Wright has acquired it. She reports that of the 450 seedlings (from a single seed pod of duPont Lavender Pink and Mrs. Boles), she has chosen but *one* as of real worth. Surely here is an example of wisdom worth emulating.

She doesn't think we should expect but one from 500 to be more "than a bet." She kept hers for study and for further crossing. She has observed it now for several years and grown many plants from it. It is now being tested by others. The conclusion seems to be that this is a better strain of an already well known variety. Mrs. Wright feels that we need more *improved* varieties instead of so many new ones.

WHAT IS YOUR GOAL?

I think we must recognize that in breeding saintpaulias there are two kinds of goals. Let's be frank—one is the fun of doing, the other that fun plus the serious purpose of producing notably improved varieties. We must make a distinction. If we are only giving ourselves pleasant occupation, records will be less important, and so will results. We will also be most hesitant about naming, most hesitant. All those lovely seedlings, most of which are very like or perhaps duplicates of existing varieties, we will just call Seedlings, and share them freely with friends and neighbors who will think of them as Mrs. Smith's violets or Aunt Mary's plants. Our venture then into cross-pollinating will have added to the sum total, never too great, of beauty and happiness in the world.

But suppose ours is a serious goal. We *intend* to develop new and better saintpaulias. Then we must prepare for a long discipline, sharpen considerably our critical faculties,—and apply them to our *own* results. We must actually begin at the end and not the beginning, for we must determine, today perhaps, the goal we hope to achieve on a tomorrow that may be five years away.

What are the improvements most needed? Here are a few: more prolific bloom and better shipping qualities in duPonts; more symmetrical growth on many good bloomers, even on that handsome monarch, Blue Boy Supreme; better whites, freer of bloom, of more interesting foliage pattern, and with less brittleness. And please, more miniatures. Some of us want beds, tables, and chairs in our houses not covered with violets. We don't like the idea of taking to the woods!

Improved color is a great and fascinating field. We need true reds, true blues, as sky blue and light "navy," and purer, deeper pinks, two-color as well as two-toned bicolors. We have lately had a number of interesting introductions with variegated blossoms. Besides Lady Geneva, there is Lady Ulery, Twinkle Girl, Dark Beauty, and Geneva Rainbow.

THE YELLOW QUESTION

And what about yellows? Saintpaulias cross-pollinated by themselves are unlikely to produce yellow, since they belong to that class of plants which lacks the essential elements to make flowers yellow. However, R. A. Brown, Jr. of Newman, Georgia, publicly expressed hope at the Cincinnati Convention in April, 1949, that he could develop yellows.

Breeders have been asked why they don't try crosses with the yellow violet. Such a mating would be as impossible as that of a black bird and canary to get a yellow black bird. The families are different. The wild yellow violet is a Violacea; the saintpaulia, a Gesneria.

Perhaps the best possibilities for yellow lie in cross-pollination with the naegelias. Two of them, N. zebrina and N. achemenoides, have some yellow in their flowers. The naegelias are of the same gesneria family as the saintpaulia, but this cousin-crossing is a tedious business, full of disappointment. So often crosses will not take or, if they do, the seed produced does not germinate. In other relatives, the gloxinias, appear the gorgeous reds likewise coveted by saintpaulia enthusiasts.

HYBRIDS AND MUTANTS

If your approach to developing better varieties is serious, you will want to tackle the subject of genetics. You may find it exciting and spend days, as I have, reading up on the subject in your local library. In Volume I of the *Standard Cyclopedia of Horticulture* by L. H. Bailey, you will find under *Breeding* a clear presentation of the factors involved. Mendel's Law of Hybrids is explained and illustrated, and a general view given of the way unit characteristics are separated and combined in cross-fertilization. Dominant traits, as the blueness of our violets, and recessive traits, as whiteness, which may not be at all apparent in F 1, or first generation, seedlings are discussed. The article differentiates between "fluctuations . . . due to the direct action of environment and . . . not inherited, and mutations, profound changes that effect the germinal cells of the organism in such a way that the changes are inherited and . . . ordinarily reproduce true to seed." Too often I fear fluctuations of African violets have all unwittingly been offered as new varieties or mutations.

The term hybrid designates "any product of a cross when the parents were noticeably distinct from each other, whether the parents belonged to different clons [vegetative groups as a Blue Girl and all the new plants from division or leaf cuttings, but not seed], races, or species. Our saintpaulia crosses are usually of hybrids on hybrids so that possibilities for variation are increased all along the line. If we cross species on species, as S. ionantha on S. diplotricha, there would probably be little *obvious* change in F 1 seedlings. The crop would closely resemble one or the other parent species and the workings of Mendel's law would be apparent. In F 2 (the second generation), considerable variation would appear.

"When hybrids have been produced between species or varieties possessing certain characters that it is desired to unite in a variety, the recombinations of characters become visible in the second generation, and it is thus among the plants of this generation of the hybrid that one should expect to find the combination of characters desired. The breeder would . . . choose for further experimentation those plants that were found to have inherited the characters which he desired to combine."

The causes of mutation, or basic change in the genes or units of inheritance, have concerned scientists for a long time. Nature's own tools include cosmic rays, ultraviolet light, radium emanations, electrical discharges, like lightning, heat, and cold, centrifugal force, pressure, vibration, shock, friction and irritation. Even insect stings may do the trick. In *Plant Magic* by James P. Haworth, the many natural possibilities are discussed, and also man's conscious use of them. We have already heard how the application of the chemical, colchicine, produced by the autumn crocus or meadow saffron, has caused doubling of flowers. We have had hints from our own experience of how brief refrigeration sometimes "shocks" a non-blooming plant into flower. Perhaps such cold might also cause a basic change. If we leave mutation to nature, it is likely that but one to ten *obvious* changes will appear in 50,000 plants. With colchicine, but one chemical possibility, man produced changes from singles to doubles in fifty percent of the seedlings treated.

The African violet is a plant easily changed. Apparently it is of adventurous spirit, and through its heredity, capable of continuous adaption. Very likely we are only at the threshold of its possibilities. In *Partner of Nature,* by the great plant breeder, Luther Burbank, an interesting statement appears that bears out our own experiences with saintpaulias:

"There are plants that are obstinate and set in their ways; . . . these have always lived narrow, restricted lives—have been bound to a fixed environment, and therefore have had no experience in changing themselves. On the other hand, all those that lend themselves easily to our efforts to change them are . . . plants that have, through the ages, been in the habit of changing their environments—of adapting themselves to different climates, soils, and moisture conditions. These . . . have in them a heredity that has stored up life experiences under varying conditions, and therefore they will learn more readily, whereas the former kind of plants—the one-type kind—have become set in their ways and don't know how to learn new ones."

This is but a glimpse of modern genetics. Even as an armchair amateur you will be fascinated. Books on the subject abound, but a good high-school botany is not a bad place to start. Bailey and Gilbert's *Plant Breeding* and the Burbank and Haworth books are other excellent possibilities.

A LITTLE BOTANY

To work with pollination, you will need to understand the botanical elements involved in cross-fertilization. The saintpaulia produces bisexual flowers, that is, each one contains both male and female organs. Study the drawings in this chapter. Then examine a flower and you will discover that besides the obvious five petals, it has three other distinct parts. (If your eyesight is fairly good you will see these plainly; if the print in your telephone book has begun to look pretty small, you will need a magnifying glass or hand lens.)

The pair of small yellow sacs in the center holds the pollen, or male fertilizing agent. These sacs are called anthers and are attached by short yellow filaments, or stamens, to the center of the flower. You will see also another filament, longer, and quite prominent. This grows out at a sharp angle from close to the pollen sacs. It is the pistil, usually the same color as the petals. However, variegated-type blossoms may not conform as to color of pistil. For instance, one white and orchid flower has an orchid pistil, although the flower is predominantly white.

The pistil is the female element. Noticeably different, it consists of three distinguishable parts. Low down at its base is a slight enlargement in which are held the immature seeds or ovules awaiting fertilization. This swelling elongates into a slender column called the style, which terminates in a tiny disk-like structure, known as the stigma. This becomes sticky after a flower has been open for a few days and continues so for several hours after blossoms fall. During this quite long interval in the plant's development, the stigma will retain grains of pollen on its surface, if you transfer them there through a process known as hand-pollination.

At the back of the flower is a green enfolding structure composed of five sepals. These form a protective envelope, first for the developing bud and later, after germination has occurred and petals have fallen, for the developing seed pod. Such a sensible arrangement!

Although each saintpaulia blossom does have these necessary male and female elements for self-fertilization, this does not commonly occur. Indeed, the way the pistil of each flower points *away* from the source of fertilizing pollen grains, would seem to indicate an effort to avoid contact. From window-sill gardeners and greenhouse people, there are reports of seed forming without hand-pollination. When a seed capsule forms indoors, it is possible that an ant or a house fly has been the pollen-carrying agent. In nature, it is also an insect or the wind which scatters pollen and brings it in touch with stigmas. However, those who have observed the saintpaulia in Tanganyika Territory, the natural habitat, report that even there, in the out-of-doors, there is but meager setting of seed.

With hand-pollination, seed is freely set. Look into the greenhouse of Fay Wilcox, for example, and you will see mature plants bearing fifty to sixty seed pods apiece. If you examine the duPont plants with capsules in early stages of development,

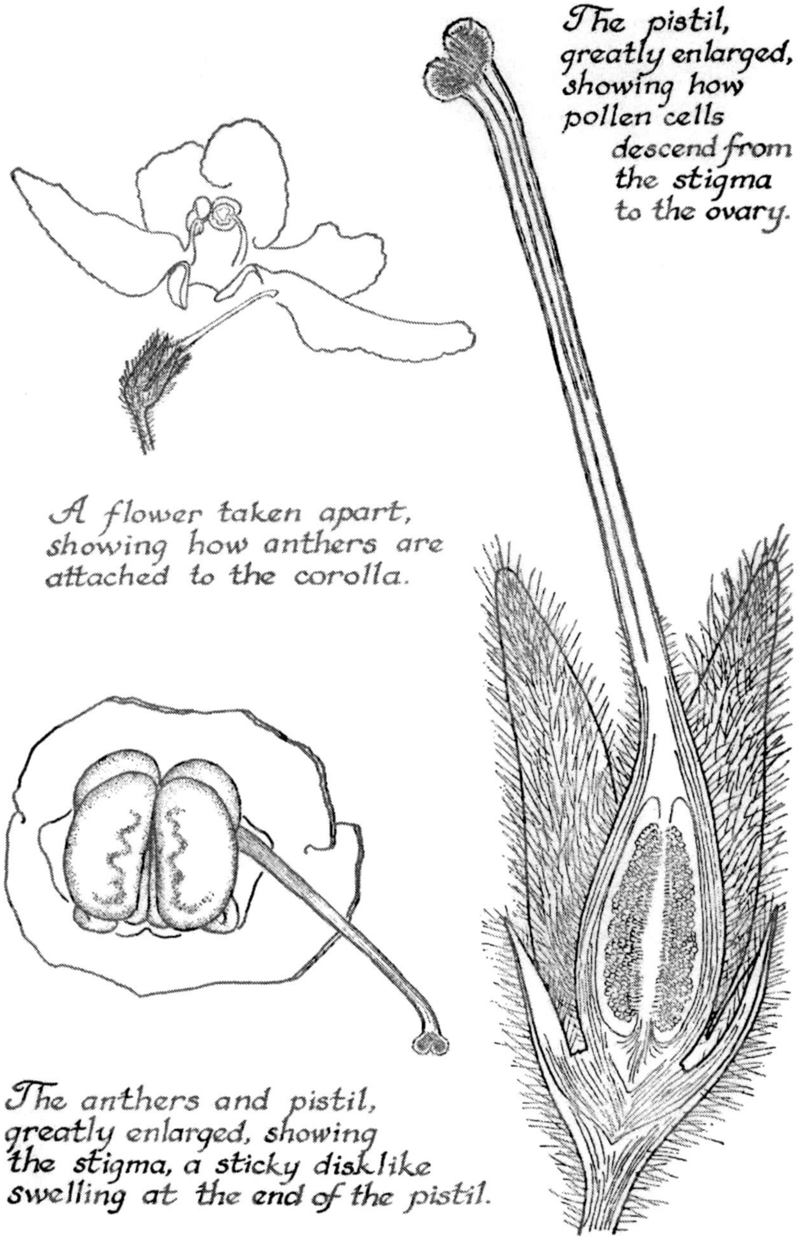
The pistil, greatly enlarged, showing how pollen cells descend from the stigma to the ovary.
A flower taken apart, showing how anthers are attached to the corolla.
The anthers and pistil, greatly enlarged, showing the stigma, a sticky disklike swelling at the end of the pistil.

Structure of a Flower

you will notice that, as you expect, they are larger than those on other varieties, but examine ripe seed pods on these same plants and you will see, as you probably didn't expect, that they are just about the same size as those on the Blue Boys, the Mentor Boys, the White Ladies, and the rest.

HOW TO HAND-POLLINATE

Now just what is this method of pollination which results in the formation of seed pods? Pollination is a term describing the reception and retention of pollen by the stigma. When a cross "takes," the ovary or seed pod at the base of the pistil begins to enlarge and finally to project beyond the protecting sepals. It requires from six to nine months for the fertilized seed to mature and ripen sufficiently for sowing. Spring pollination usually produces seed in about six months, while summer and autumn pollination requires eight to nine months.

Commercial growers in their pollination program usually start by removing, if possible even before the bud opens, unwanted pollen-bearing anthers from the female parent, so as to avoid self-fertilization. Only occasionally will anthers burst and shed pollen naturally. As a rule you have to open the small sacs, but to guard against the occasional burst, it is wise to remove pollen sacs from all seed parents. Use pollen from the same plant or from another plant of the same variety to get seed for plants of the same variety. Use pollen from one variety on the stigma of ˉnother to get a cross. You can transfer the pollen from the nther of the chosen male parent to the stigma of the chosen emale by one of several methods.

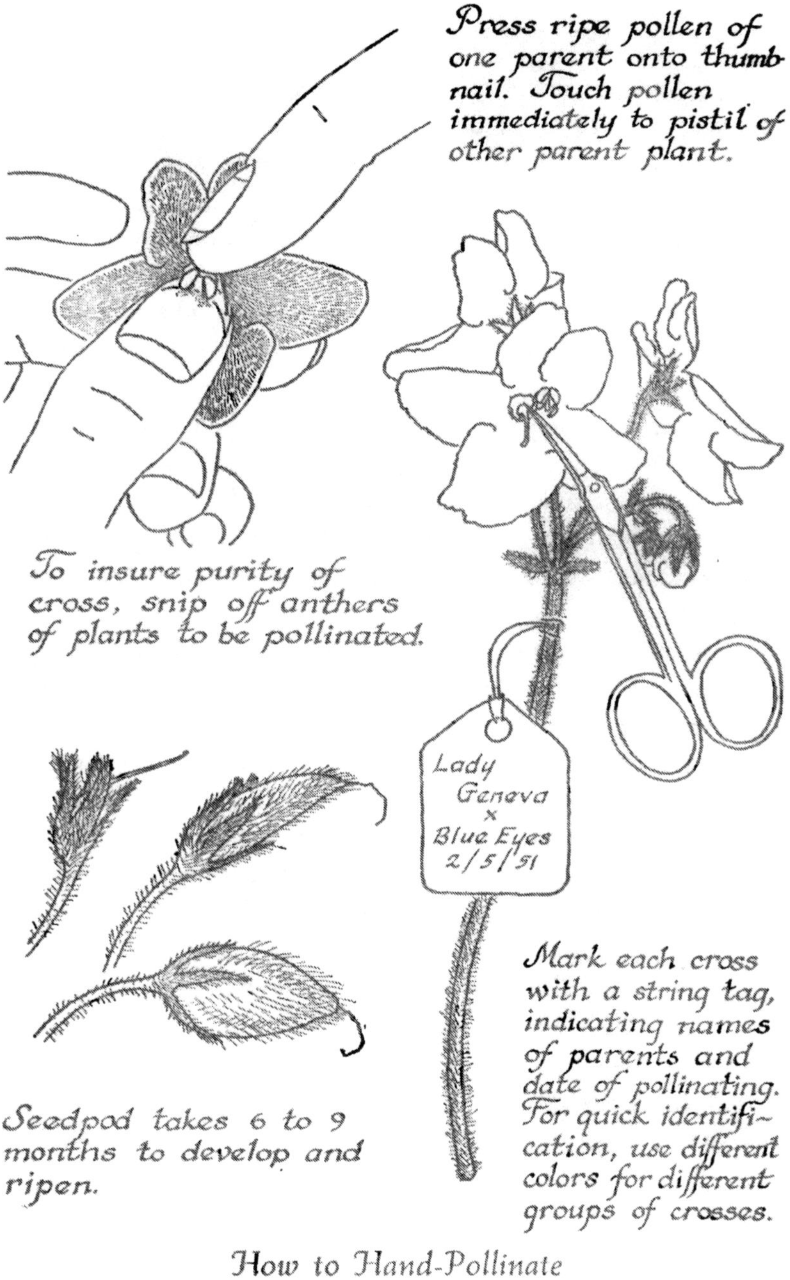
Press ripe pollen of one parent onto thumbnail. Touch pollen immediately to pistil of other parent plant.
To insure purity of cross, snip off anthers of plants to be pollinated.
Lady Geneva × Blue Eyes 2/5/51
Seedpod takes 6 to 9 months to develop and ripen.
Mark each cross with a string tag, indicating names of parents and date of pollinating. For quick identification, use different colors for different groups of crosses.

How to Hand-Pollinate

Fay Wilcox cuts a tiny section in the yellow anthers of the selected male parent, lets the pollen dust fall on her thumbnail, and then brushes it over the disklike stigma of the selected female flowers. The process could hardly be simpler. You may prefer to remove the anthers, carry them to the other parent and insert the stigma into the snipped pollen sacs, or to transfer pollen by means of a small paintbrush. By whatever method, the end result should be stigmas yellow with pollen grains.

The best stage for pollinating is when a flower appears mature —not old, not newly opened, but fully developed. You will have to observe your plants closely, and experiment a little to determine the best time for collecting pollen. It has long viability. There is evidence that pollen mailed great distances has still produced successful crosses, and that a year's storage does not destroy it.

When the pollen grains come in contact with the stigma, fertilization does not immediately take place. First the protoplasm around the pollen cells elongates. It bores down through the style (which supports the stigma), forming a pollen tube. The male elements within the tube advance, as the tube elongates, until the tube enters the ovule. Then the sperms are released, come into contact with the ovules or eggs in the ovary, and fertilize them.

Fertilized plants should be tagged so as to have an easy, readable record always at hand. Small string tags with the name of the cross, as White Lady x Blue Boy (put seed parent first), are useful, particularly if you tie on tags of a different color for each pollen parent. A numbered record is shown at the end of this chapter. An actual record should be kept for each cross, if in the end you want to know what you have and how it has behaved.

SEED PLANTS AND THE CROP

Grow plants which are producing seed somewhat on the dry side, and insure a better than usual circulation of air. Examine daily for rotted petioles. These could start softening of the pedicels bearing seed pods. A close atmosphere may result in the softening of seed pods before they are mature. If this occurs, snip them off, and spread them out to dry in a warm dry place. So treated they may mature even though away from the plant. There is disagreement as to whether it is necessary to remove flowers from plants with developing seed pods. I think the seeding is more likely to detract from the flowering than vice versa.

Completely developed seed pods shrivel, dry, and turn brown on the plant. When they look "done," remove them and take along the pedicel. The usual practice is to let the capsules dry for a month to six weeks, but you can plant at once, or you can wait for as long as a year. "The vitality of these tiny seeds is amazing," writes Fay Wilcox. "Some varieties germinate very unevenly. We have had seed from Pink Beauty that started to germinate in a couple of weeks and continued to do so for four months."

When the pods are dried, split open and sow the seed, or store the pods until you are ready in labeled envelopes, or small medicine bottles or jars. I like those well-capped plastic bottles my pill-dispenser now supplies. Keep the stored seeds in a slightly cool place. A temperature of 60 to 65 degrees F. is fine.

Now what can you expect from the seeds of your carefully made crosses? Just about anything. If you are familiar with Mendel's law you may be looking for a certain number of the offspring to resemble one parent, a certain number the other, and some to combine the parents' characteristics, both the dominant and the recessive ones. Keep in mind, however, that these results can be expected only with crosses made on *species,* and who today could be sure of working with a species of ionantha? Only, I should think, if a plant could be obtained from the original African locale. More than likely your crosses will deal with *varieties,* so there are infinite and unpredictable possibilities. Actually every cross represents a small miracle, and who is not filled with awe at this intimate revelation of Nature's wise designs?

If yours has been a serious effort, perhaps a project involving considerable expense, you will examine your developing plants and the first flowers with concern, if not anxiety. Do I have *anything?* you will ask, meaning anything promising for introduction. If you decide you have, grow it vegetatively two or three times to see if it comes true. (Hybrids do not come true from seed.) You would also do well to self-fertilize a few plants to see what the seedlings are like. Perhaps you have an important mutant (which does come true from seed), and not a hybrid at all.

HOW TO REGISTER NEW VARIETIES

The next question must be, is it worth registering? If your plants are *as good as* or *almost the same as* acknowledged varieties, even the best of them, please do not register. So much near duplication and exact duplication already exists that it is too bad to increase nomenclature problems. If something really better, a better strain, for instance, or something undoubtedly new, appears by all means plan to develop as much stock for introduction as you can.

Then proceed to register. Write to the Committee on Registration of the African Violet Society of America for a Registration Form. The address (1951-53) is Layton Lake, Penns Grove, New Jersey. Return the filled-out form to the Committee Chairman, Neil C. Miller, and your application will be published in the *African Violet Magazine*. (There is no charge for this service and you do not need to be a member of the Society to use it, though, of course, you will want to be.)

If after two notices at six-month intervals, your variety is accepted, the registration will become permanent. There is a possibility it will be contested. The name may already have been used, or another grower may have established a prior claim, or someone else may have produced the same variety you have. Don't feel too bad if this happens. Scientific discoveries, to which men have devoted their lives, have been simultaneously announced, even in distant quarters of the globe. If your variety is challenged in writing, as is required, the decision rests with the Registration Committee. All this is fair and square and, as an ardent saintpaulia fan, you will undoubtedly be grateful for this means of giving your variety legal status, or if it does not deserve it, of being saved from compounding present confusion. Indeed, no project of the African Violet Society—and there are many good ones—has been of more value than this effort to sort out varieties.

HOW TO RECORD A CROSS

#11 Mrs. Boles x Lavender Pink duPont—F 1.

3/1/48	Cross-pollinated plant.
3/14	Signs cross has taken.
10/5	Seed pod looked mushy. Removed with a long stem, placed in a small dish in the china closet. Kept at room temperature.
1/4/49	Sowed seeds in ⅔ sterilized peatmoss, ⅓ vermiculite.
1/22	Germination just visible.
1/30	Watered with warm Hyponex water (¼ teaspoonful to 1 quart of water).
2/7	Hyponex again.
3/20	Transplanted largest seedlings to covered dish (continued transplanting until 6/15/49).
5/15	Transplanted first seedlings to 2½'s in soil mixture.
7/28	First flower. Medium blue resembling seed parent. Other seedlings showing buds.
12/10	F 2. Selfed the selected seedling (a nice dark blue). (Leaf cuttings from this seedling reproduced true through 3 vegetative reproductions, which took time.)
10/1/50	F 3. Seeds planted.
Result:	A dark seedling apparently a better dark blue du Pont than present one—improved foliage and fatter blossom of good substance and fine color. No name yet.

BRIEF GUIDANCE TO POLLINATION

1. Select parents each with some outstanding characteristic—perhaps take pollen from a parent with fine flowers and select a seed parent for quality foliage.
2. Pollinate, preferably toward spring. Be sure the stigma is sticky.
3. Snip open pollen sacs of selected male parent with a manicure scissors, and let pollen fall on your thumbnail.
4. Rub pollen on stigma of selected female parent.
5. In 7 to 14 days look for swelling of ovaries.
6. In 6 weeks, expect well-developed pods or capsules extending beyond sepals.
7. In 6 to 9 months remove seed pods, as dried, shriveled condition indicates maturity.
8. Let pods dry in a warm place for 4 to 6 weeks after gathering, or sow seed at once.
9. Sow preferably toward spring, or at least after the "turn of the year." A year for the cycle is good, if you can wait that long. What to expect? Anything!

CHAPTER FOUR

From Seed to Flower

There is no unbelief;
Whoever plants a seed beneath the sod
And waits to see it push away the clod,
He trusts in God.

LIZZIE YORK CASE

Whenever I think about seeds, I recall these lines. Few gardeners ever become so familiar with the seed-to-flower process that they are not always a little thrilled over what happens. I know that for me seed sowing will always be an adventure.

To have the fun of growing African violets from seed, it is not necessary to pollinate your own plants. Today you can purchase from commercial growers fine strains of seeds, even seed from specific crosses, perhaps of the varieties you particularly admire. You will find that you can have blooming-sized plants from the dust-fine seed quite as soon as from plants grown from "putting down a leaf," sometimes sooner. It depends on the varieties involved, and also on the growing conditions that obtain at a specific time.

SOIL FOR SOWING

You can sow seeds in any one of a variety of special mixtures or "mediums" and get good results. What is important is that the mixture you prepare should have water-holding capacity, yet be light and well drained. Well-worked garden soil, a little peatmoss, and a liberal quantity of sand will fill the requirements. Or you may prefer to combine half-and-half vermiculite and peatmoss. This is a popular mix with a number of fans.

Fay Wilcox has successfully used vermiculite alone, also vermiculite and powdered sphagnum moss. She is now trying out a combination of $\frac{1}{3}$ sand and $\frac{2}{3}$ granulated peatmoss.

With mixtures including soil, it is wise to sterilize by steam or baking, or in the greenhouse with a chemical to prevent damping off of seedlings. It is most important that nematodes be banished. Since these apparently attack germinating seeds and seedlings, they may be the cause of a poor stand.

POT, PAN, OR DISH

For seed sowing use an ordinary flowerpot or shallower bulb pan with a sheet of glass for a cover; or sow in a covered glass baking dish or casserole. The glass cover makes pot or dish act like a minature greenhouse. An evenly moist condition, so essential to germination and early growth, is maintained. (Some favor covered fruit jars for seed sowing, but I find using them almost an acrobatic feat.) Arrange the crocking and drainage layer for pot or bulb pan just as you would for a plant (see Chapter One). Then fill in the soil mixture, making it fine as fine. It's easy to sift the top inch of soil through a kitchen strainer —a little coarser than a tea strainer—if you are working with only a few pots.

If you use a covered dish, spread an inch layer of small stones or bits of charcoal over the bottom, as in the drawing. Charcoal has the advantage of keeping the soil sweet. Let the mixed peatmoss and vermiculite soak up water overnight. Then drain and squeeze them fairly dry and lightly pat them 1½ to 2 inches deep, depending on the dish used, over the stones or charcoal.

Sprinkle the seeds ever so lightly over the carefully prepared soil in pot or dish. After sowing, firm the soil gently; it is not necessary to cover with additional soil. Then put the sheet of glass or glass cover in place and move to a warm, light, sunny place. If the temperature ranges from 75 to 85 degrees F., germination will start in 12 to 14 days, and continue over several weeks, or even for a period of months, depending on the varieties sown. Once it starts, move the seedlings out of the sun but to a good light window, and as close to the glass as possible. Good light means good growth.

Keep the growing medium *barely damp, but never wet.* If moisture collects on the glass, remove it for a few minutes, dry it, and then replace. Plantings in glass dishes must be watered from above. Use a houseplant syringe, whose fine mist will moisten without flooding or make a little hole in one corner of the planting and water through this. Since glass coverings prevent much evaporation, you will find very little extra watering necessary. Water plantings in porous pots from below. Let them stand in water until the top soil feels just moist.

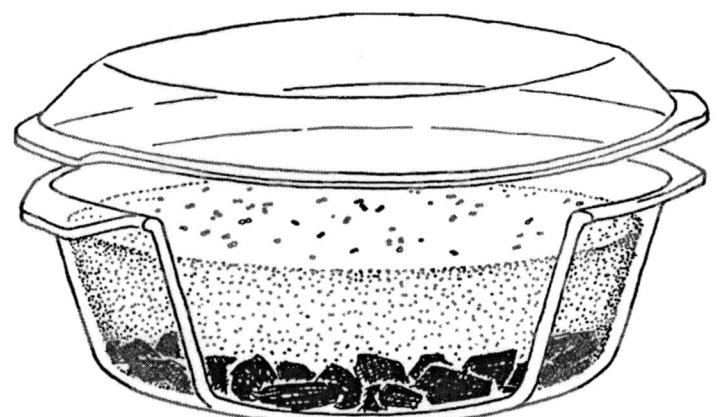

Glass casserole used for germinating. Cover the bottom with charcoal, then fill in with a half-and-half mixture of vermiculite, and peatmoss, soaked in water overnight and squeezed dry.

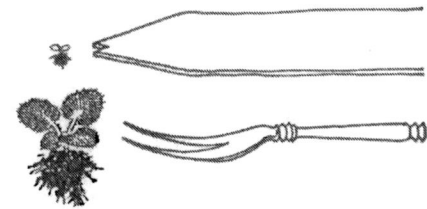

Useful transplanting tools — a notched plant label and a small fork.

Seedlings appear in about 3 weeks, and are ready to transplant when they are ½ inch high. Shift them to 2- or 2½-inch pots, in a mixture of equal parts loam, peatmoss, and sand, or in a commercially prepared mixture.

Seeds and Seedlings

SIGNS OF LIFE

At first, that is in 12 to 14 days, and continuing for perhaps 4 months, little green spears will appear. These will unfold cotyledons or seed leaves. When you see them, start watering about once a week with a mild solution of your favorite plant food dissolved in lukewarm water. Hyponex is fine for this purpose. Allow ¼ teaspoon to 1 quart of water. Be watchful of damping off just after germination. If plants are too wet now, are in drafts, or get too little air, this rotting off due to fungous growth may start. If you see signs of trouble—mold or a "cobwebby look"—water right off with some fungicide, such as Fermate, ¼ teaspoon to 2 cups of warm water.

Fermate mixes better if you do it like flour for gravy. First make a paste of the Fermate and a little water. Then add the rest of the water. (This is a duPont product and generally available. It is also good to immerse leaf cuttings in before they are planted, or you can dip the ends in the dry powder, mixed half and half with talc. If small areas of rot occur on stems or leaves or leaf cuttings, apply a little dry Fermate with a small paintbrush to the affected parts. This may very well check the trouble.)

When seedlings have 3 or 4 leaves and are about half an inch high, it is time for new quarters. Use a 2- or 2½-inch pot (measure across top), for each, or set seedlings 2 inches apart in a flat or bulb pan. Avoid making seedlings compete for light, air, and nourishment. It's better to transplant over a long period than to wait to do the job all at once.

Move the smartest youngsters the first day. If seedlings are allowed to stay where they started too long, petioles grow twisted and lengthy, the plant starts out spindly, and is unlikely ever to have a sturdy, healthy appearance.

Fill the small pots or flats for the seedlings with half pure leafmold and half garden soil. Or plant in whatever soil mixture you have found successful for your larger plants. Be sure to sterilize whatever you use, unless it is a package of soil already sterilized by the concern that sold it. After seedlings take hold and growth is obvious, apply weak liquid fertilizer once a week.

TRANSPLANTING

The first transplanting—4 to 6 weeks after germination—is somewhat tedious. You don't want to move the seedlings "bare root." Each should carry along a tiny ball of the soil in which the seed germinated. A pickle fork seems the best tool to me (and at long last a use for this item), or you can just pry out each seedling by inserting a toothpick or curved grapefruit knife well down in the soil below it. Take along all the roots there are; don't break off a single strand.

Move your fine crop of potted seedlings into good light. A north window is fine at this point. They won't want even a glimpse of sun for another two months, or until they are well acclimated to growing alone. When they are established in the pots or flats—you will be able to tell from the way they start showing off with new leaves—you can move them to a location of filtered sunlight. Start *preventive* spraying with Optox,

NNOR, or whatever you prefer. Repeat as you do for mature violets, about once a month.

In 6 to 9 months, the first exciting blooms will open. Promptness depends on varieties, season of the year, and growing conditions. Just think, at this point you don't even know what you are going to get! Maybe you will have a plant as lovely as one of the Fringettes, as spectacular as Lady Geneva, as distinctive in foliage as Blue Girl or Ruffles. Nobody knows yet. Exciting, isn't it?

BRIEF GUIDANCE ON SOWING

1. Prepare a light, moisture-holding mixture—soil, sand, and peatmoss; or half-and-half vermiculite and peatmoss; or vermiculite and powdered sphagnum moss.

2. Use flower pot or bulb pan and cover with a sheet of glass, or sow in a casserole with a cover.

3. Sow on moist soil surface and press seed down very lightly.

4. Put on glass cover.

5. Strive for a 75 to 85 degree F. temperature until after germination, then the usual 70 to 72 degrees is fine.

6. Water just enough to maintain a barely moist condition, perhaps only once a week.

7. When first green appears, start watering once a week, sparingly, with a weak fertilizer dissolved in *warm* water.

8. In 4 to 6 weeks, before crowding, transplant to 2's or 2½'s (pots), or to flats (2 inches apart). Use half-and-half leafmold and garden soil, or equal parts loam, peatmoss, and sand, sterilized.

9. Keep in a light place until 2 months after transplanting, or when new leaves indicate plants are well established. Then move to filtered sunshine.

10. Start monthly preventative spraying 2 weeks after transplanting.

11. Expect first flowers in 6 to 9 months.

CHAPTER FIVE

Greenhouse Wisdom

> *For the earth has till now produced nothing more beautiful than flowers.*
> *They have completed the conquest of the globe.*
> MAURICE MAETERLINCK

Investment in a greenhouse is certainly an investment in fun. How nice it is to move your saintpaulias from the necessary restrictions of a dwelling to a home meant for them alone. Even a small 8- by 10-foot glasshouse will accommodate a large and representative collection, especially if you put shelves up everywhere, so every precious inch of space can be used. For, of course, though you will have plenty of room the *day* you move, six months later you know as well as I what has happened to it.

In any case a greenhouse means space for hybridizing and propagating, space for flats of seedlings, opportunity to have some large mature plants in pans. A small, well-run setup might even maintain itself with a limited amount of selling. Perhaps you could specialize in just a few hard-to-get varieties, and advertise your stock in a local paper.

Your greenhouse of saintpaulias might also serve your other

interests in church, school, or community. You can grow plants for fairs and fêtes and make your charitable contribution that way. Buyers at benefits always flock to the plant booth and, in general, they won't care whether you sell them named varieties or "a nice blue." Incidentally such donations are also a good way to spread joy with a hoard of seedlings, from which you have made selections in your breeding program. You can't possibly keep all of them, even if you successfully sowed but one podful, and there are so many people who can be made happy with just a few violets.

The man or woman interested in plants and wanting a small profitable business would be wise to consider building a greenhouse and raising saintpaulias under controlled conditions of light, heat, and ventilation. Some of our best growers today were hobbyists yesterday. They saw opportunity all around them, especially in the increasing demand for the less common varieties of doubles, the crinkled- and ruffled-leaved types, the various bicolors and variegateds, and the plants with flowers of unusual shadings or different habits of growth. A few years ago commercial houses catered to the demands of florists rather than to those of collectors. Today they serve both and carry tremendous stocks sometimes offering more than 100 different varieties. Even so "the little fellow" still has a good chance, for local hobbyists and collectors—and travelers too—like to see what they are buying and enjoy an opportunity for personal selection.

If you are inexperienced in running a greenhouse, the following brief generalities on management will help you through the first experimental year of your perhaps mysterious venture. After that time, you will have arrived at an almost automatic schedule with heating, ventilating, and watering no longer matters of crisis or special concern.

HEATING

It may be that you can proceed economically and heat the glasshouse attached to your dwelling from the same boiler that heats your house, if this boiler is for either steam or hot water. Electric heat is the favorite for small hobby greenhouses, in sections where rates permit. It is mercifully easy to operate. Where there is natural gas, that's fine, oil heat also. Select what is easiest, and, of course, cheapest for you. If you decide on electricity, you can have those compact heaters that set underneath the benches. Warm air is circulated by a small fan. The thermostatic control is accurate and hardly varies one degree all night.

At first, it will help with routine decisions if you realize that the aim is to run a greenhouse so that it will approximate the conditions of a natural day. Changes of atmosphere should be gradual with about a 10-degree drop in temperature at night—just as it occurs in nature when the sun goes down. Through the day a 75-degree F. temperature is suitable, though daytime heat, provided there is ventilation, may unavoidably run as high as 85 degrees without harming saintpaulias. At night, 60 to 65 degrees is low enough. Violets suffer at temperatures below that: leaves curl and turn light green, and growth and bloom are noticeably checked.

SHADING

With African violets, it is essential to shade the greenhouse from early spring to fall. Dim the light through these seven to eight brightest months by maintaining on the glass a coat of whitewash or of shading paste, which comes in green or white. Or you might follow the example of one large saintpaulia firm and use a shading mixture of chalk whiting, a material used in preparing some of the cheaper grades of paint. This is obtainable through most paint and hardware stores.

In addition to the whitewash or similar coating on the glass, cheesecloth or tobacco-cloth may be hung inside the greenhouse. This will not only shade but also protect plants during periods of ventilation from the drip of rain or snow and help to avoid spotting of foliage. It can be applied or removed at will and, being flexible, makes it easier for you to keep up with the weather during shifty spring and fall seasons.

Roller slats are another possibility. They can be more exactly regulated and are nicer looking than anything else. They are necessarily more expensive than dabbing on whitewash and hanging a cloud of cheesecloth.

Of course, too much shading is to be avoided. Cornell University recommends for saintpaulias 1000 foot-candles minimum and 1500 foot maximum. We all know that too much shading will reduce growth and flower development; too little will result in burning.

THE ART OF WATERING

Plan to water your plants in the morning as the temperature of the day rises and vents can be opened. Mid-morning is a good time except on very hot summer days. Then 8 to 8:30 A.M. is better while foliage is cool, and the sun is low. Thus burn is avoided.

Plants should not be watered at night, when condensation on foliage is likely to cause fungous trouble. Even in bright winter weather, once a day always suffices; in dull weather less is needed. In December and January every third or fourth day is enough. In spring and fall, watering is usually necessary only on alternate days. In summer, saintpaulias will need more. Take a look at them about 10 A.M. and again at 2 P.M. Very likely you will find plants in 2's and 3's thirsty both times; the morning watering should be enough for larger plants. It is important not to risk dryness to the point where foliage wilts. Whenever the weather is dark and evaporation is slow, as is likely through December and January, take particular care to moisten only the soil and not the foliage. Overwatering during sunless stretches may start an attack of leaf splotch, while water on foliage in bright weather causes burning.

The best method is to go over the plants, pot by pot, watering them safely at the rim from a slow-running nozzle or, if the number is not too extensive, you can use a dipper. It is important that water be unchilled. Take care that it keeps to room temperature or a little above. Even in the heat of summer, hose water gets very cold. Temper it with enough hot water from the boiler to take off the chill, or if your greenhouse is small, keep a large tub of water under a bench. This will hold an adequate supply to dip out for your needs, and it will always be of agreeable room temperature.

Various experiments have been tried with sub-irrigation, now that regular wooden benches can be made watertight with a preparation called Kendex, but greenhouse men differ as to the benefits. Here are two expert opinions. Ernest Chabot, author of *Greenhouse Gardening for Everyone,* says:

"I like sub-irrigation for saintpaulias but do not recommend automatic watering. Plants get too wet. It is best to set pots right on top of sand or cinders and not plunge."

C. W. Fischer, jr. reports: "Our benches are covered with coarse gravel and at present our watering is done by hose, and overhead. The pots are watered individually with a slow stream of warm water. We have tried, with relative success, to use a constant water-level bench. However, the difficulties of rotten leaves, where petioles rest on moist pot rims, and of soluble salts rising to the soil surface, must be coped with. Basically we think the constant water level or some method of bottom watering will be a great thing for violet growers once it is *perfected* under practical conditions. Our future plans are being formulated on this assumption."

GREENHOUSE FEEDING

If you have progressed to greenhouse culture, you should have your soil tested so you can be intelligent about potting mixtures and plant foods. There are a number of sources of soil-test information, so get in touch with your county agent, state agricultural experiment station, or the department of floriculture or horticulture at your state college. Let one of them help you.

Before sending a soil sample, find out just where it should go. My own inquiry, as a Connecticut resident, went to Hartford, from which I received explicit directions as to the method of sampling and mailing, with a form to fill out to insure my giving full information.

You can base *your* program of extra feedings on the recommendations given for *your* particular conditions. At the Tinari Floral Gardens, Hyponex and Proliferol are used alternately and applied through a hose-nozzle device that mixes the fertilizer from a separate receptacle into the water. Fischer Flowers also use Hyponex at double strength—2 pounds per 100 gallons—every 2 weeks, except during the winter months. Feeding is started when plants are "established," that is, about 3 or 4 weeks after well-rooted cuttings have been potted, and repeated so often because Atlantic City soil is understandably sandy, and readily leaches. Fischer's feed with a slow stream from a hose, but with no nozzle attachments. "The fertilizer is dissolved in a 600-gallon tank in our basement. This tank can be connected to the water lines in any of our greenhouses. When we are ready to feed a selected house, we disconnect the regular water tank and connect the feed tank into that line. A little centrifugal pump does the rest, and we water-feed right through the hose. We use this same tank for heating water for plain watering. We simply fill it with the approximate quantity of water necessary and run a steam hose (tapped off the main), into the water. When the water feels lukewarm (no thermometer is used), the steam is shut off, and the water pumped into the particular line we are using."

PEST AND DISEASE CONTROL

A clean and tidy greenhouse is one of the best possible checks to insect and disease. Pick off discolored leaves and gather up the constantly discarded flowers of saintpaulias. Where bits of foliage or other vegetation collect and decay on benches or walks, disease finds an inspiring breeding ground. It is all I can do when I walk through a greenhouse and see these danger spots not to ask for a paper bag and impolitely start a gathering and burning project all on my own. I strongly recommend discarding badly infested plants. Too often people try to save bad ones and only spread more disease through the house. Of course, if all your plants have caught something you have to try "cures" or else throw out everything and begin all over again. And that's expensive!

In the well-run commercial or home greenhouse, there is constant house cleaning but in a piecemeal way. Unlike many other greenhouse crops, roses for instance, there is no definite beginning and end to violets, no opportunity to move everything out at once—bushes and soil—and fumigate before starting a new crop. Instead, in a large setup of violets, two or three days a week might be regularly devoted to cleaning up beds and making new ones. After a group of new plants has been potted, a clean fresh bench or bed is prepared for them, and this goes on all the time. If a group of plants "breaks down" for no good sensible reason, out it should go. Ruthless as this practice may seem, it means protection for thousands of other plants. The collector will sometimes clean house by washing pots with soap and water and a disinfectant, polish glass, and do a bit of painting. In the little house hazards are less, procedure more casual.

Greenhouse controls have three aspects: (1) soil sterilization or fumigation for nematodes; (2) general pest control; and (3) disease control.

SOIL STERILIZATION

With proper equipment the soil in a greenhouse can be sterilized by steam. Under pressure, steam is forced through the soil in perforated or porous tiles till soil remains at 180 to 200° F. for 30 minutes. This heat apparently disposes of beetle grubs, nematodes, various soil-borne diseases, and most other harmful bacteria and fungi, as well as weeds and weed seeds. It is a cheap, quick method well adapted to *commercial* use.

With fumigation, a "tear gas," such as Larvacide is used. If you have a *small* greenhouse, you can get a one-pound "dispenser bottle," convenient for pouring or sprinkling, with a graduated scale on the label indicating the fluid ounces. Allow ¾ pound per pound of soil. If the soil is dry, wet it down 4 or 5 days ahead. (Organisms are more active in dry soils.) Then screen the soil before treating to avoid lumpiness. Work at a temperature no lower than 60 degrees F. and up to 85 degrees. You won't need to wear a mask if you work in the open air.

This is the method: Procure a drum, garbage can, or small bin. Spread about 6 inches of soil over the bottom. On the dispenser, check the proper amount of Larvacide for the amount of soil to be treated. Pour ⅓ of the required amount over the 6-inch layer; quickly cover with more soil to the half way point; pour over this another ⅓; fill soil in to within 6 inches of top; apply remainder of estimated amount; spread the rest of the soil and cover tightly—and fast. The gas generates as it goes down. You want it to act *in* the soil and not be dissipated in the air, hence the speed.

If the container you are using has no cover, water the soil surface after treatment and cover with wet burlap bags, or a wet piece of carpet to confine the fumes. Thicknesses of newspaper will also do the trick. Keep the covers wet for 24 hours. Then the soil can be aerated.

For a large greenhouse where much soil is needed, or perhaps a quantity sold, Larvacide is obtained in cylinders and special injectors are used which accurately measure the amount of each application. A full face mask is advisable for large-scale operations and again, a warm room. In one greenhouse 5 layers of soil are treated at once in a pit 5 x 15 x 7 feet. Each 12-inch layer is treated and covered as a unit so that the soil can be uncovered and used, layer by layer, without exposing the whole amount.

After about 7 to 10 days, the top layer is uncovered, and the soil thoroughly turned over. Then it is aired for 2 weeks more. After that time, Larvacide-treated soil is ready for use. If not contaminated, it can be counted on to remain "sterile" for 5 to 6 months.

Dowfume is another excellent possibility. You can follow one collector's tested procedure with it: to 1 bushel *damp* leafmold or soil use 6 tablespoons Dowfume G. Place leafmold or soil in lard can, or other container with a cover. Punch 6 holes in the leafmold or soil, tunneling them down to the bottom of the can. Pour 1 tablespoon Dowfume G into each hole. Cover openings *lightly* with the leafmold or soil. Do not *pack* holes. Place cover on container and do not disturb for 1 week. Pour treated contents into a wooden box or onto a tarpaulin, and *air for 5 to 6 weeks*. Be thorough about this aeration. Sniff the soil before using. If there is the least little whiff of something alien, air another week. Let soil get rained on and turn and turn again to insure airing. Do this job outdoors. (Other easy methods of sterilization for small quantities of soil are discussed page 125ff.)

Larvacide, Soilfume, D-D, Dowfume N and W 40, Dowfume G, and other products require different periods of coverage and different periods of aeration before it is safe to plant in soil treated by them. All this is discussed with reference to these available trade products in an excellent pamphlet, *Soil Fumigation for Control of Nematodes*, published in April 1948 by the Plant Industry Station of the United States Department of Agriculture at Beltsville, Maryland. It will be supplied on request. Each manufacturer also offers full directions for his specific product.

PEST CONTROL

In the commercial greenhouse, pest control is now largely dependent on Parathion aerosols. These are not toy balloons but highly dangerous chemical bodies safe only in the hands of the well informed, the well guided, or the experienced. From the Bureau of Entomology, also at Beltsville, is obtainable a report

(E-759, October, 1948) on *Parathion in Aerosols for the Control of Pests on Greenhouse Ornamentals*.

Parathion as a *cure-all* should be used about once weekly for 3 treatments. This will catch mites in all phases. *Control* is then achieved by a "bombing" once every 5 weeks, which will keep nicely at bay cyclamen mite, mealy bug, spiders, aphids, white fly, and practically all other greenhouse insects.

Parathion makes it unnecessary to selenate soil. Indeed selenium should not be used, since the combination of the two causes severe plant injury. Sulphur is also dangerous with parathion. If you use sulphur for mildew control, wait for 7 days to use parathion. If you *have* used parathion, wait for 7 days to use sulphur, or substitute for it malachite green (McClellan 3), which can be used at the same time as parathion, if there is simultaneous need for mildew control.

Greenhouse men who have used parathion swear by it. I will not attempt to give the elaborate instructions and necessary warnings here. These can be obtained from the manufacturer. After studying them, I feel that, if I were using parathion, I should require some one of sound judgment and keen eyesight —preferably fond of me—to keep me in constant view from the outside and make sure that I continued to maintain the perpendicular! I don't wonder the wives of greenhouse men worry on Parathion Day!

If you have a home greenhouse, don't attempt to use parathion. It emphatically is not recommended for amateur use, first because it is so dangerous, and second because each aerosol covers 200,000 cubic feet, and with a dispersal rate of 4 seconds per 1000 cubic feet, it is impossible correctly to guess the amount for a small house. An overdose would result in burn and injury. Furthermore, some $26.00 worth of equipment is needed. Even small commercial greenhouses are better treated with Plantfume 103 smoke generators. These require no wearing of gas masks and are suited to 5000 cubic feet or more, but not less.

For the home greenhouse new chemical products, Dithio and K 6451, are being perfected. They will be safer for us to use and promise to be very effective, but are not yet available. Good results have also been achieved with 15 percent wettable parathion, sold as Planthion. Used as a dip, it controls cyclamen mite, mealy bug, and various other insects. Read the directions and note that Planthion is POISONOUS. Don't get a drop of the liquid on your skin or inhale the powder or fumes. Work outdoors and wear rubber gloves for the dip.

For the solution dissolve 1 ounce, with 2 teaspoons of a soap powder like Dreft or Vel, in 4 gallons of warm water . . . a rather deep, medium-sized galvanized or aluminum tub makes the job easy. Invert the plant, while supporting the soil firmly with your fingers. Dip to submerge entire plant, but not necessarily the entire pot, though there is no harm in soaking the soil. Dry dipped plants in the shade. For a sure clean-up of mite dip twice, at intervals, one month apart. Throw away the solution.

Decide upon a regular spray program to coincide with your convenience and the health of the saintpaulias. Hit-or-miss spraying when you at last find time is wasteful in every way, since it fails to deter, and deterring pests and diseases is far easier than controlling them. In fact, control in some cases is just about impossible. When mealy bug or mite reach the stage of serious infestation, your procedure is all too likely to be—discard.

It is wise to spray the *home greenhouse* once a month, more or less, as you find it necessary. Choose a cloudy morning and carefully use one of the all-purpose preparations according to the manufacturer's directions. NNOR, Optox, Protexall, or Yamtox, as well as a number of others, are good. It is better to alternate materials than to depend entirely on one. An all-purpose spray regularly applied should keep saintpaulias free of mealy bug, aphids, and mite. And for real mite insurance, there is always sodium selenate for the greenhouse, to be used as explained in Chapter Six.

DISEASE CONTROL

The third aspect of greenhouse control—that of disease—is largely dependent on general regulations of watering and ventilating. Mildew for instance is mainly controlled by uniform temperatures. In spring and fall when outside and greenhouse temperatures are almost the same, it's a good idea to be a little wasteful of fuel and keep the greenhouse about 5 degrees warmer than outdoors. This prevents condensation, the prime spreader of disease, and so is a natural mildew control.

For disease control, when heat is on, Fischer's rely on a paste of Fermate, which is spread very thinly over the pipes. This decomposes with the heat and liberates just the right amount of sulphur. They first tried sulphur alone but found the treatment too drastic.

Occasionally, especially during late spring and summer, a Fermate *spray* is a good thing for a large commercial greenhouse. It is a preventative of crown rot when weeks of dull or rainy weather make fungous troubles likely. Use 1 to 2 tablespoons to 1 gallon of water, preparing a paste of the powder and a small quantity of water before adding the whole amount of liquid. Fermate may discolor flowers and leaves a little, but that's better than an onslaught of crown rot. The Tinari's feel that spraying with Fermate is "a necessity."

Of course, African violets are plants of very tender foliage. They are easily damaged by many types of sprays, although the plants themselves show an inherent power to recover from spray injury. Still the cure seems worse than the curse when, to insure health, a whole house of plants is spotted and the flowers browned. Under such conditions, commercial value is temporarily gone. However, saintpaulias are only profitable if nematodes in the soil and mites on the foliage, the two most potent enemies, are controlled, so the commercial grower must maintain a pest-free greenhouse. To proceed intelligently, he should have his name on various state and government mailing lists so that he can keep abreast of modern experimentation. Besides the pamphlets already suggested, information on aerosols and on sodium selenate compounds for mite control, can be obtained from, to mention but one firm, Plant Products Corporation, Kennedy Avenue, Blue Point, New York.

THE WAY TO VENTILATION

Proper ventilation of a greenhouse, large or small, is most important. Although saintpaulias like it warm, they do not thrive in close "dead" air. Even through the winter a fresh, alive atmosphere must be maintained. One sniff will tell you. It should *smell* fresh. Only during periods of extreme cold and storm should you leave ventilators closed for 24 hours.

Spring and fall are critical times when there may be considerable dampness in the greenhouse. During these seasons it is advisable to leave the ventilators open a bit to maintain the proper humidity, even when the heat is on. This practice also helps to maintain the required temperature. Although the day temperature is kept as near 75 degrees F. as possible, on summer days the heat will soar dangerously above this, if ventilators are not open to admit cooler air. In cold weather, fresh air is usually admitted from the roof so there will not be a draft on the plants. The cloth, hung underneath the ventilators, helps to prevent this. It is important from September to December to "crack" ventilation, whenever weather permits.

Ventilation may also help to maintain humidity, if the greenhouse gets dry, due to artificial heat. Sprinkling walks with water has long been considered good practice, although some recent research indicates that the resulting humidity rise is transitory and that, within 15 minutes of syringing, humidity returns to the original level. Perhaps the increase for 15 minutes is worth while, also the benefit can be prolonged, if moisture-holding materials are present. In Tennessee, where summer greenhouse temperatures are sometimes hazardous for violets, Alma Wright tells how she placed "3 inches of river sand over the floor. Over this was spread finely crushed limestone. It was piled deep under the benches. Then the floor (the stones and sand), was wet down thoroughly. What a difference the cooler, damper air made . . . Now the moisture stayed.

"On the benches galvanized pans, 3 inches deep, were filled with a coarse grade of vermiculite to a 2-inch depth, and over this was placed an inch of crushed stone. When this was wet down and the plants placed on the stones, the humidity was increased at their level." A Humidiguide indicated when humidity was too low and showed when an extra spraying with the hose was needed. Mrs. Wright also used *five* layers of tobacco-cloth for shading the roof and sides, and every afternoon at 3 on hot, dry days, this too was sprayed with the hose, and from the cloth, cooling moisture was dispensed for a long time.

To avoid temperature extremes, automatic electric ventilation, thermostatically controlled, has been developed for small greenhouses. By this means the ventilators open when the sun hits the greenhouse and heats it above the required temperature. They close when the sun goes under clouds or goes down at the end of the day.

Without automatic control, ventilation requires fairly regular attention along with that judgment which comes with experience. Through the summer and early fall keep the ventilators open all the time, day and night, unless the weather is unseasonably cool or storm threatens. Then, of course, ventilators must be closed to avoid the damage of a ripping wind. When night temperatures drop toward the thirties, close the ventilators tightly at sundown. Then open them in the morning as sunshine warms the house.

BRIEF GUIDANCE FOR THE HOBBY GREENHOUSE

Here are a few month-by-month suggestions. Spray for insect and disease control only as you find you must. It may not be necessary every month.

SEPTEMBER. Actually this is the beginning of the greenhouse year, not January. Now days grow cool, and heat, the most important aspect of greenhouse procedure, must be turned on. Heat automatically if you can with oil, coal, or a stoker, thermostatically controlled. Then the temperature will stay right where you set it.

In any case inspect the heating system now to see that it is in fine working condition well before you need it.

Sometimes September is surprising. A sudden cold spell is no time to get in the repair man or to send away for replacement of equipment. The forehanded, of course, tend to the heating system in June. In case you didn't, clean the smoke pipe right away, oil the hinges, check the insulation on the boiler, change the water, and vent air from the heating coils. If there are pumps and motors in connection with the system, oil them, or have them checked by an electrician to make sure they are in good operating order.

When night temperatures can no longer be definitely maintained at 60 to 65 degrees F., or nights keep persistently damp and cool so that the greenhouse has a "creepy" atmosphere early each morning, turn on the heat. Do this even if you seem to be wasting fuel by keeping the ventilators open through most of the day. Cold and dampness are not the saintpaulia's friends, and you must take care now that plants do not get off to a poor start for the winter.

The exact date for turning on the heat even in a given locality varies considerably and often as much as two to three weeks from one year to another.

Even without heat keep ventilators open through most of the day. Never be hidebound by schedule. Judge the conditions as they are, not as the calendar indicates they should be.

Naturally heat is not needed so soon in the South as in the North and East. Once you turn it on in your greenhouse, however, watch the humidity. To maintain good bloom in the fall, when so many shows are held, keep your mind on it. If humidity falls too suddenly, or too far, blooms will fall as well.

Begin to check the light. Fall shows require good bloom, and plants need plenty now that days are beginning to be shorter. Be watchful, for your violets may tell you too late that they can't set buds without more light. Remove a little of the paint or other covering on the glass just as soon as it seems necessary. Don't let shorter days creep up on you unawares.

Inspect the glass for leaks. After the first hard rain is a good time. Make the little repairs early and you won't have to make big ones later. A leaky pane can cause a lot of damage in cold, stormy weather.

Selenate for fall mite protection, or if you favor other than selenate, get to it (page 118ff.) This is a time to be most careful.

Watch out for slugs on the walls of the greenhouse, on bottoms or sides of pots, or anywhere that moisture collects. If undetected, they will live over the winter and be most annoying.

Use one of the poisonous, commercial slug-baits. You may be amazed at the number you get.

Prepare a generous quantity of your favorite soil mixture well before frost. Sterilize or fumigate for nematode control. Toward the end of this month spray once with Fermate, or spread pipes thinly with it as a check to disease.

Feed all established plants, on the little-and-often system. Give more when plants are growing well during bright weather. Make up a stock solution of your favorite brand, and have it handy. Regular feeding means larger flowers of finer color—and more of them—and handsomer leaves too. With Hyponex, mix 4 teaspoons to 1 quart of water for a stock solution; for application, use 1 cup of "stock" to 1 gallon of water.

OCTOBER. Gradually decrease the amount of water given to plants as days grow shorter and the daytime heat of the house stays closer to a 75-degree F. average. Watering by the end of the month, or sooner, should be on an alternate-day schedule. However, give enough through those farewell weeks of Indian Summer, when afternoons may be very hot indeed. This is "touch-and-go" time.

Continue to watch the amount of light. Remove more of the covering on the glass, or if you did not start to last month, start now. Toward the month's end the glass must be clear, or plants will suffer severely, since days are so much shorter now.

Take down screens and screen doors and store them, unless you live in the South. There wait well into November, if fall afternoons still incline to be warm.

Close the ventilators at night. Open them, more or less fully, as weather indicates, about 10 o'clock each morning.

Give less plant food, if weeks of prolonged dull weather begin to slow up plant growth. Be watchful of ventilation during these "heavy" days.

As last spring's leaves develop new plant colonies, pot these up separately in 2's or 3's.

NOVEMBER. Continue the winter-maintenance program now established. Spray regularly. Be vigilant. If any insect attack gets ahead of you, spray or dust frequently until it is cleaned up.

Dull days are here now and for perhaps 8 weeks to come, so avoid overwatering. Every third or fourth day may suffice, but examine daily to be sure.

Be sure to pay attention to the diminishing light and be watchful also on days of shifting sunshine. It will be summertime inside your greenhouse, if you have cleaned up the glass by this time, and on some days, even this late, the sun may be too bright. Your plants will continue to bloom well, if light is regulated.

Ventilate judiciously so as not to chill.

Sow seed at any time ripe pods are available.

DECEMBER, JANUARY. These are the two worst months for pest and disease. Crack ventilators as often as weather permits. Avoid stale air.

If stems of larger leaves become jellylike, consider if the house is being kept too damp and too cool, or whether consistent watering from below is causing a deposit of fertilizer salts on the soil surface. This will rot petioles that touch it. If rot is in evidence, (1) flush soil with two or three thorough top waterings; (2) cover pipes thinly with a paste of Fermate which, as it oxidizes, will destroy fungous spores; (3) pick off hopelessly damaged growth but give a chance for recovery where injury is slight.

Send as Christmas presents to your saintpaulia friends, leaves from some of your choicest varieties (though, of course, not of patented kinds). Let the outside wrappings be festive, but inside observe the practicalities of packing with the leaf dry and the stem moist. Label: "Open at once; don't wait till Christmas!"

The New Year is a fine time for starting a new crop of seedlings. They will be ready to go outside in late May or June, and so not take up valuable greenhouse space in summer. Through the summer their blooms will indicate what can be discarded before cold weather.

FEBRUARY, MARCH. As days lengthen, African violets burgeon. Feed with a freer hand now, if growth is developing and more and more buds are in evidence with the advancing year.

Shade more, as it is necessary on bright winter mornings. Even in February a bright, warm week may occur, particularly in the South. Have a light covering ready. Bleached plants do not win prizes at spring shows.

Take leaf cuttings in abundance. They seem to root more quickly now than at any other season. Leaves taken at this time should mean fine 3-inch pot plants for autumn selling, when everyone gets interested in houseplants again.

In dull, muggy weather, be particularly mindful of greenhouse cleanliness. Pick off imperfect leaves. Gather faded flowers so freely dropped each day. A clean greenhouse means healthy stock.

Better selenate again in February. For some reason this is another bad time for mite.

In March start grooming plants for spring shows. Perfection doesn't just happen!

APRIL, MAY. Ventilate more freely. Shade more carefully. Water more abundantly.

Take as many leaf cuttings as space and time permit. Do a little hybridizing, being careful to keep accurate records so you'll know what you have when at last you get it!

Water newly planted leaf cuttings freely, and fertilize them.

Be ready to dim the increasing light with paint or a cloth covering. Three hours of strong sunshine on foliage can destroy a year's good care. Shift plants about and turn them, if light is coming from any particular side.

Put up screens at windows and doors. They are essential to keep out bugs, especially moths and night prowlers when you make an evening visit. Screens are also an aid to ventilation.

Don't be in too great a hurry to turn off the heat. It may still be necessary at night all through May.

Check over varieties. If you want new ones to replace older ones which should be discarded, get out your catalogs and order before hot weather makes it hard for travelers.

Pot up seedlings and young plants for fall selection. Spring is the time to start getting some fall beauties ready.

Spray or dip plants back from a show before returning them to the greenhouse.

Replenish soil around older plants to pep them up.

Clean house a bit. Scrubbed pots and shining glass are good health insurance.

Spare a few sprays of saintpaulias to arrange in a little vase for your desk with true violet leaves and a few yellow primroses and stars-of-Bethlehem from the outdoor garden.

JUNE. Turn off the heat, weather permitting, which it usually does.

Keep the ventilators open during the day, but only cracked at night.

Water daily, as necessary, but still observe the precautions of keeping the water warm.

Give extra humidity as needed. Wet down the floors morning and night.

Better selenate again for summer safety. Try to pick a time of cool weather. Selenation and high temperatures are a dangerous combination.

Watch that light!

Select a few specimen plants for the veranda, but out of wind and sun. Place ferns and vines among them. Don't be afraid to plunge outdoors some of the extras, or the not-too-rare plants. Out of sun and wind, they will flourish.

JULY, AUGUST. Take a vacation from your own violets but don't hesitate to journey in a direction where other saintpaulias grow—which now is everywhere. Hobbyists enjoy meeting other hobbyists, to compare notes on culture, convictions on varieties.

But leave in charge of your greenhouse someone of at least average saintpaulia intelligence. And with him or her, leave a *written* list of directions. If temperatures soar, wetting down walks and frequent waterings are essential.

Before you go, remove bloom stalks, particularly if you have had trouble with molding foliage from faded blossoms resting on it. If you can gauge the removal of two weeks' bloom, that won't hurt your plants at all, only give them a needed rest. (The nurse in charge can hardly be counted on for such devotion.) Your plants will then welcome your return with a blaze of glory.

Be inhospitable to slugs. They are circulating around outside again and casting envious glances at the cool, moist atmosphere of your greenhouse. Keep the screen door closed and some snail-bait about.

Through the summer, water early in the morning, shade to prevent bleaching, ventilate freely, and guard humidity. Low humidity results in little bloom, and that of small size and substance, as well as dull, droopy foliage. Summer care is just as important as that of winter.

If you stay home, don't keep so busy you forget to have fun. Growing saintpaulias, lots of them, is a grand business. Enjoy it!

QUARANTINE REGULATIONS

If you are going in for saintpaulias commercially and live in a horticultural zone, quarantined because of Japanese beetle infestation, your shipments will have to be made under government procedure and inspection. Write to your county agricultural agent for particulars. If you do not know who he is, write to the Department of Agriculture in the capital city of your state for information. Then you can arrange to have a representative of the department advise on fumigating the house where saintpaulias are grown for shipping. You must also sterilize potting soil so that it will be free of grubs. Then periodically he will inspect to be sure regulations are being regarded and give you, if requirements are met, a certificate to permit shipping.

Saintpaulia leaves, which carry no earth, may be sent free of inspection. Plants destined for intershipping zones in already infested "beetle areas" also need no inspection. (In addition to Japanese beetle trouble some of the southern states are infested with the white-fringed beetle. All shippers living in infested areas must also comply with the quarantine regulations pertaining to this insect.) See also page 163.

If all this seems unduly irksome to you, it is only because you have never seen the Japanese beetle working untrammeled and at the height of his powers. I once lived near Riverton, New Jersey, where the beetles were first introduced to this country. It was nothing to see them turn a velvet golf green into a piece of old hay in a few days. Trees were defoliated. Roses ruined.

Beetle control is necessary, so do your part and be patient with the inspector who has to do his!

CHAPTER SIX

Evil Elements—Pest and Disease

"We sometimes had those little rubs which Providence sends to enhance the value of its favours."

OLIVER GOLDSMITH

Saintpaulias appear to be prone to many troubles. Indeed a whole book might be devoted to what these small charmers can get and what we should do about it when they do. Only it isn't a book I should like to write—or read. The literature of pest and disease always makes me miserable. I feel the whole matter should be crisply, though wisely, dealt with. We must, of course, know the problems and *plan* to cope with them, not wait until they are upon us. But let us not be obsessed by them! I hope enthusiasts will always be able to meet without spending *more than half* their time on nematodes, mites, crown rots, and such. I maintain African violets should go on being *fun!*

Actually, it is quite possible to grow African violets successfully over a period of years and only rarely have to deal with pest or disease. Especially if plants are all home-reared and kept culturally content is there little danger of ailments. Like a happy child, a happy plant is usually a healthy one. One collector who

EVIL ELEMENTS—PEST AND DISEASE

has some two hundred plants reports but two specimens attacked by mealy bug in seven years, about three with crown rot, and only two with mite—none now that she practices isolation of unknowns.

If you receive plants from outside sources—greenhouse or home—it is really most important to grow them apart from your other plants for about two months. It hardly takes this long to diagnose mite, yet if a newly purchased plant had recently been infested, the trouble could go unnoticed for about this length of time before newly formed leaves unfurled to confirm your suspicions. After two months you can be sure, and safely let new plants mingle with your own healthy stock. In tending violets during the trial period, wash your hands before you go near other plants, even to water them.

I do not mean to infer that florist's stock is likely to be unhealthy or infested. It is just that an occasional plant, which he has every reason to believe to be in first-rate condition, will sometimes, particularly under less ideal home conditions, become a prey to a disease or pest, which greenhouse conditions kept in abeyance. If plants are purchased directly from an African violet grower, there is practically no danger of getting an infested specimen. All the experienced growers today maintain an almost clinical cleanliness in their greenhouses. They use only sterilized soil. They fumigate and they spray. They are as anxious as you to have only healthy violets and avoid epidemics which, once started, might ruin thousands of valuable plants. Indeed each grower guards jealously—and at great expense—his hard-won reputation for "clean stock."

There are three precautions for you to observe if you would avoid saintpaulia grief:

1. *Beware of strangers.* Keep new plants away from your others for 6 to 8 weeks. If no trouble develops in that time—particularly nematode or mite trouble—then give a welcome, but not before.

During this test period, water the newcomer from a pitcher kept for it alone, and be sure to wash your hands before watering or working with your other plants. Don't be a carrier. Remember Typhoid Mary!

2. *Segregate for observation.* If one of your plants gets a "different" look, let it live alone in another room till you can estimate how big that little difference is. Maybe your care will prevent an epidemic of mass illness.

3. *Prevent trouble.* You know the old ounce that is worth "a pound of cure"? Be mindful of it. Don't bring cut flowers from garden or greenhouse near your violets. Delphinium, amaryllis, gladiolus, in particular, may carry thrip. Plant only in sterilized soil and use an "all-purpose" spray thoroughly once a month, or oftener, if necessary. Then most likely you won't ever meet up with the *dramatis personae* of this discussion.

Here then are the diseases and pests I hope you will never encounter, but which you should really know so that you can recognize their presence by the earliest possible symptoms.

CYCLAMEN MITE

Symptoms: In the early stages foliage in the center of the crown looks lighter than the rest. Perhaps when you first suspect

EVIL ELEMENTS—PEST AND DISEASE

trouble, the small leaves are already a sickly gray or yellowish green. Buds, blossoms, and blossom stems are distorted. These last may thicken abnormally or be considerably shorter than usual. Growth in general is dwarfed. Hairiness is more pronounced than on healthy plants, and leaves tend to cup *upward* and be quite brittle. Buds may drop prematurely. No pest will be visible. In later stages, the central crown will have been destroyed and new "desperation" growth will be pushing out at the side of the center.

Diagnosis: Doubtless this is cyclamen mite, particularly if the season is fall, winter, or early spring, and conditions are somewhat damp—as in a house where the heater has been allowed to go out and cold weather has returned. To check your suspicions, carefully examine your plant with a hand lens. Look well into the convolutions of the youngest leaves. There you may see the minute offender or some egg masses. Younger plants will be more severely damaged, since all their leaves are attacked. Older plants have the reserve of their strong outer leaves on which mites cannot subsist.

What to Do: Treat with NNOR, Optox, Endopest, sodium selenate, or in the commercial greenhouse with parathion or Plantfume 103 smoke generators. You may be able to save most of your plants, if tissues are not too badly damaged. It will take a few weeks to clean up a light infestation, but even at that it may be about 2 months before plants are well recovered—and look it. All your plants may not be infested. Mite is unlikely to travel to pots kept 3 inches apart, nor will it live on a window sill or other surface away from plant tissues for 24 hours. If one part of your collection is still mite-free, take every precaution to keep it so. Segregate the suspect violets and water from a vessel kept just for them. Wash your hands before touching other plants. Since mites spread by contact, let me repeat, be sure *you* are not the carrier.

NNOR may be used as a spray or dip—1 teaspoon to 1 gallon of lukewarm water, *mixed well*. If you spray, put plants in the bathtub (NNOR won't damage porcelain), and spray forcefully and thoroughly, reaching the deep center of the crown, and both upper and under surfaces of leaves. If necessary, remove a few leaves to open up the tight center area to the spray.

For the dip, mix the solution in a vessel large enough for the plant to be entirely submerged. Let it remain under water until the soil is soaked and air bubbles stop rising. If you are treating a number of plants, the solution may get too dirty to do the whole lot in the one mixture. You will then have to prepare more than one batch of dip.

Let sprayed or dipped plants dry in a shaded place before returning them to direct light. If too many particles of soil adhere to foliage, spray lightly with clear, lukewarm water right after the dip.

Repeat the dip or spray weekly until you have given 3 clean-up treatments. Then spray or dip once a month as part of your program of preventive care.

Optox—1 ounce or about 2 tablespoons to 3 gallons of lukewarm water—can be used in the same way as NNOR, that is 3 times at weekly intervals, and then once a month. This timing destroys the eggs laid by the last crop of adults.

EVIL ELEMENTS—PEST AND DISEASE

Endopest is a dry dust which comes in its own handy applicator. You may prefer to dust. Use it every 4 days for 1 month. Then remove any traces of it from the foliage with a warm-water shower. When dusting a plant, try to coat all surfaces *evenly and lightly*. Cover the crown as thoroughly as possible, but don't let great drifts of dust settle there.

Reconditioning: Plants that have been damaged by cyclamen mite have a very sick look indeed, even after mite has been dispatched. Usually damaged tissue is even more damaged by the rigors of the dip. A breaking or wilting point may develop low down on the petiole so that many large leaves fall. You cannot help this, so be philosophic, knowing that the alternative was probably the loss of the infected plant. With tweezers, pick out the withered center leaves. Remove others that are severely damaged or distorted, but don't remove *all* the foliage until some new appears. Plants breathe through their leaves and even impaired ones are better than none. Suckers will appear at the side of the old crown. Select one to train toward the center to make a new crown. Cut off the others.

When the plant seems convalescent and well on the way to new life, repot it. Cut off dead or brown roots. These were not directly attacked by the mite, but have reacted to the general illness. Use a clean pot (disinfect by dipping in boiling water, if it was used before), and probably a smaller one, since the root system is now likely to be considerably reduced. Set the plant a little farther down in the soil than it was before to conceal the lower bareness of the new sucker you are training.

Withhold plant food and grow "on the dry side" until complete recovery is assured and the shock of transplanting sustained.

Prevention: Regular monthly spraying or dusting with NNOR, Optox, or Endopest, to mention but three brands, should keep your plants free of cyclamen mite. Or you can use sodium selenate, as outlined below, and be certain of mite protection for a period of 3 to 5 months, supplementing with spraying for varieties slow to react to selenate.

SODIUM SELENATE SOIL TREATMENT FOR MITE

Sodium selenate is a "systemic," an insecticide absorbed by mites (also red spider, mealy bugs, aphids, but not thrips), when they "scratch" the surface of the tender center leaves and "drink" the plant juices, thus producing the typical scarred foliage and distorted growth. Systemics less lethal to man and animal, and with other improvements, are coming but be careful with Systox (also known as E-1059), OMPA, and Pestox 3. Use sodium selenate only if you are willing to observe the precautions necessary in handling a POISON. It is deadly to plants, animals, and people, and must be kept out of reach of children and all irresponsible persons. Throw any residue solution down a drain. Never dispose of it in a garden or near plants grown for food. There are two methods of application, the Standard, which is very strong, and the Extra Dilute Method, which I recommend. It has proved successful for many amateurs, who loudly sing its praises. (And it's no more hazardous than common iodine or lysol.)

EVIL ELEMENTS—PEST AND DISEASE

For the Extra Dilute Method, dissolve ⅛ teaspoon (1 gram) of the pure selenate in 3 gallons of water. (Measure the selenate loosely; do not pack.) Select for the solution a container which can be closed afterwards, so you can store the extra for future treatments after labeling it POISON.

Properly used, with due respect for its advantages and disadvantages, selenate is excellent. Improperly used, it can and will kill plants as well as mites. Even with a severe infestation it is wise to make haste slowly and repeat weak doses, rather than to try for a knock-out, burn foliage, and very likely destroy your plants.

A commercial preparation, Kapsulate, offers sodium selenate in capsule form for inserting in the soil of each pot. The capsule is dissolved by watering and the selenate carried through the soil. Or capsules can be dissolved and a solution applied.

BYLAWS OF SELENATION

1. Mix ⅛ teaspoon pure sodium selenate, measured loosely, in 3 gallons water.

2. Apply through a V-shaped hole made in the soil of each plant close to the pot rim, or apply from the bottom, filling the saucer with the recommended dosage for the size of the pot.

3. Allow 2 fluid ounces (¼ cup) for a 4-inch or larger pot; 1 fluid ounce for 3-inch or smaller pots. Use a glass measuring cup with a lip for pouring.

4. Be sure the soil is *wet* before selenating. Soak the day or night before until water runs freely through the soil and flushes

out all plant food and salts, both hazards in the selenate treatment.

5. Avoid heavy fertilizing for 1 month before and 1 month after selenating.

6. Avoid letting plants get too hot for several days after selenation; 60 to 65 degrees F. is best.

7. Avoid spilling solution on leaves or petioles. It burns them. If you have an accident, quickly pour warm water over foliage.

8. To *clean up* mite, treat 3 times, at 10-day intervals.

9. To *prevent* mite, treat twice at 10-day intervals, and repeat in 3 to 5 months.

10. Treat *older* plants with caution, but do give them selenate protection, since mite lives in the growing crown and flower buds, even if it does not feed on older leaves. Repeat the 2-ounce dose, no larger, even for very large plants, 3 or 4 times at 10-day intervals, instead of the usual twice. (Younger plants receive selenate more safely than older ones.)

11. Treat only growing established plants. Let a shifted plant wait 30 days before selenation; let a considerably disturbed *transplant* wait longer.

12. Give travelers, plants that have "been through shipping," a 30-day breather. It takes that long for them to recover from possible shock and to get used to a new environment. Selenate then, even if you have purchased plants already selenated.

13. If you are coping with a serious attack of mite, continue all-purpose spraying weekly, until enough selenate has been absorbed for a plant to fight back without the spray assistance.

14. Avoid over-selenating. Because a little sodium selenate is

EVIL ELEMENTS—PEST AND DISEASE

good for a plant, it does not follow that a lot is better. Proceed cautiously in going beyond the minimum dosage.

BROAD MITE

Symptoms: Foliage curls *down* more than usual and the general look of debility occurs in late spring, summer, or early fall. There is no noticeable increase in hairiness, nor is any pest in evidence.

Diagnosis: Broad mite is probably at work. This one attacks lower surfaces of leaves, causing a curling *down*. (Cyclamen mite generally distorts and causes the leaves to curl up.) The difference in diagnosis is worth while, since broad mite is easier to get rid of.

Cure: Dust thoroughly and lightly with fine powdered sulphur (or use Endopest, if you have it). Be sure to cover the underside of the leaves. Dust again in 4 days, and then again in 4 or 5 days. It takes just about that time to produce the new generation, which you must also catch.

Prevention: Your regular dusting or spraying program for cyclamen mite control will take care of this kind too.

STUNT

Symptoms: Similar to those of cyclamen mite. Leaves are shorter and broader than normal ones of a given variety. As Dr.

Floyd F. Smith points out: "They appear thickened, quite turgid and brittle. The marginal crenations are obliterated or reduced. The margins are rolled up, exposing the lighter green lower surface." Younger leaves seem more affected than older ones. All look shinier because the length of the hairs has been reduced two-thirds. Petioles are shorter.

Diagnosis: All this adds up to a "pathological condition called stunt. It disfigures, but does not destroy."

What to Do: There is no cure. Plants must be discarded, since stunt persists "in the progeny of affected plants propagated by leaf cuttings or divisions." Before parting with a choice specimen, however, be sure it is not just another victim of cyclamen mite. See what results are possible with one of the treatments for that. If growth becomes normal again, rejoice. Mite is bad enough, but stunt is worse.

Prevention: Wise and regular care will probably go far to prevent stunt unless you have been unfortunate enough to have plants of diseased parentage.

NEMATODES

Symptoms: Loss of vigor and general debility in a plant may be ascribed to starvation, over- or under-watering, too much or too little light, or the wrong fertilizer. However, if foliage loses its good green color, becomes pale and dull, and outer leaves droop, if young leaves emerge already damaged and sustain the injury through life, if flowers are fewer and those borne have a lack-luster look, if there has been a procession of other ills—mealy bug, black flies, springtails, or some such—if there has been violent reaction to selenium, if the low center or "plant stalk" feels soft and the plant seems "rocky" in the pot, if several or all of these conditions occur, you may as well prepare yourself for the worst and turn the sufferer out of the pot so that you can examine roots. Small pulpy enlargements, swellings to two or three times normal diameters (rather than knots), these, and a galled, spongy condition of the stalk at the soil line, or an "enlarged, rough, and calloused" stem (signs of resistance to trouble) fill in but one picture.

Diagnosis: Root-nematode is indicated. This is the hated fifth columnist of the saintpaulia underworld. The fine, threadlike, parasitic worms destroy indirectly for they interfere with the life processes by which a plant supports itself. The damage they do often appears to be root-rot, crown rot or galled stems. Because root-nematode attack is so difficult to diagnose, plants are often treated for other ills, and many eventually die.

The damaging process is mostly done by females migrating through the soil until a rootlet is reached. Tissue is pierced and entry made to the very center. Then they go into a sedentary condition, feed, and grow, remaining for life in the one spot. After piercing the tissue, nematodes inject a secretion which causes several plant cells to enlarge and become "giant or nectarial cells." These produce food for the larvae which become adults in 3 or 4 weeks. Each female lays 400 or more eggs which create more nectarial cells in the same place or not far away—a few inches or at most a foot.

If with a razor blade you will slice through the stem near a rotted area and examine it under a hand lens, you will find "pearly white dots." These are the root nematodes. You will notice also on examining the whole area with the lens that the outer covering of the stem has been stripped off and that a brown moist area encircles it. You may see fungous gnats, reddish mites, wiggle tails, and tiny garden centipedes. They are profiting by the damage done, and are not the primary cause of it.

Nematodes cause so much trouble by interfering with the circulatory system of the plant. Sometimes the plant resists stoppage and areas swell to keep a passage open. That is the explanation of the rough thickened stems.

What to Do: To date there is no cure. Parathion offers possibilities which may be realized in the future, but not now. Even cutting off the good upper portions of plants that have suffered from nematodes will not save them. They may reroot in water only to succumb later as the nematodes reappear. Infested plants should be thrown away where no soil from them can touch other saintpaulia soil or that used for garden or greenhouse, for once infested, always infested.

Prevention: Sterilize the soil mixture you use for African violets, not just the loam but all elements such as the sand and fertilizer which are to be included. There are two methods for doing this in small quantities.

EVIL ELEMENTS—PEST AND DISEASE

SOIL STERILIZATION

I no longer recommend the boiling-water method. It has proved inadequate because the water cools too quickly to be completely safe. Perhaps if the treatment were repeated several times, it would be more effective. Baking is certainly better. Sterilizing in a pressure cooker has also proved successful. It is clean and easy to manage.

Baking-Pan Method: Spread the soil mixture out in a shallow pan and bake it in an oven for 1 hour at a temperature of 180 degrees F. (Or you can put a medium-sized potato in the center of the pan and bake the soil until the potato is done). Do not overdo this baking business. The soil must not be heated to a point where no beneficial bacteria remain and it can only support plant roots, not nourish them. (I believe that those who recommend 450 degrees F. for baking must fertilize heavily afterwards, since the high heat destroys so much.) After the soil cools, stir it well to aerate. Then allow it to *stand* for three days before planting.

Fumigation Method: Destroy undesirable soil organisms by applying one of the commercial fumigants, such as Larvacide, or Dowfume, both available in small quantities. (See details for use of either on page 94ff.)

Formaldehyde dust is also a possibility. Allow 1 pound to 1 bushel of soil, spread 5 inches deep in a box. (a) With a spoon scatter the dust over the dry, well-pulverized soil. (b) Stir to mix thoroughly. (c) With a sprinkling can wet the surface to dissolve the powder and seal in the fumes. (d) Cover the box of soil tightly by wrapping in thicknesses of wet newspaper, carpet, or an old piece of blanket, and leave for 3 days. (e) Stir to aerate soil and do not use until not the faintest whiff of formaldehyde remains.

Pressure-Canner or Pressure-Cooker Method: Set the wire rack in place and pour in about half an inch of water. For a 14-quart canner, prepare a 12-quart can of dry soil. Place it in the canner, fasten the top as usual, and process for 1 hour at 15-pounds pressure. When the pressure is reduced, lift out the pail. The soil will be steaming and moist, and can be used as soon as it has cooled to room temperature. It is not necessary to wait for it to dry out.

In the smaller pressure cooker, also use a can to prevent the soil from messing up the utensil. Allow 30 minutes at 15-pounds pressure. A 1-pound coffee can is useful in the small cooker.

There will be some odor from the steaming soil, but it vanishes quickly. If any fertilizers are in the soil mixture, however, the steaming will hardly be fragrant, so if you can do the job on a basement stove, it would be a good idea.

The Easy Purchase Method: You can also buy sterilized soil from special dealers or growers of African violets. If yours is a small collection, the "packaged product" is surely your answer.

APHIDS OR PLANT LICE

Symptoms: Clusters of tiny, usually black, insects on succulent new growth.

Diagnosis: Very likely these are aphids or plant lice, which debilitate by sucking out vital juices.

What to Do: If the attack is light and only just starting spray on three successive days with lukewarm water, or hold the plant on its side under a slow-running faucet, carefully turning so that the stream of water cleanses all the affected growth. If the attack is severe and the plant is "simply crawling," an unlikely condition unless other affairs of life have prevented regular care and inspection, as they sometimes must, use a spray or dip of one of the commercial products which destroy sucking insects—Black Leaf 40, NNOR, or Optox.

Prevention: Spray regularly once a month with your favorite all-purpose product. Then you will very likely never have aphids—or mealy bug either. There is evidence that mite too is thus deterred. Treating soil with sodium selenate—primarily for mites—also discourages aphids.

MEALY BUG

Symptoms: Plants look dusty, and flower stems and leaves have a grayish, webby appearance. Deep in the crown and on the underside of leaves, cottony clusters will be visible.

Diagnosis: This is mealy bug, which usually moves in on plants ailing from some other cause, although it may appear on healthy plants too. It exhausts and, if undetected and not eliminated, destroys plants by extracting cell sap through sucking mouth parts. Mealy bug presents one of the more obvious saintpaulia problems. Symptoms can hardly be confusing.

What to Do: Single-crown plants are more easily cleaned up than multiple-crown specimens, which offer just that many more hiding places. In light attacks piercing each bug with a needle, pen point, or toothpick will, if patience survives the process, get a plant clean in the course of weeks, or even months. Or you can apply an alcohol-dipped swab or small paintbrush to the mealy bugs and also gently rub the spot where they have been. Inspect and treat a plant every few days until all the newly hatched offenders have been destroyed. After applying alcohol, hold each plant on its side under a slow running faucet of warm water. This will wash off the excess, which has a dangerously drying effect on the tissues of the brittle stems and leaves of saintpaulia.

Severe attacks of mealy bug require sterner measures. To reach safely all the folds of dense brittle foliage dip the plants in NNOR or Optox solution, as you do for cyclamen mite.

Prevention: The monthly spraying with either of the above also deters mealy bug. Since badly infested plants may have to be discarded, you will be so wise to *avoid* rather than to try to clean up mealy bug. Watch out for contamination from gift plants or other houseplants which may carry mealy bug. It can also be air-borne from shrubbery outside an open window.

Amazon Purple Prince   Snow Prince   Tinari's Pink Luster

Lady Geneva
Pink Beauty
Violet Beauty

Sailor Girl, Variegated
Red King
Neptune

Apollo
Mauve Fringette
Amazon Blue Eyes

DuPont Lavender Pink
Tear Drop
Fantasy

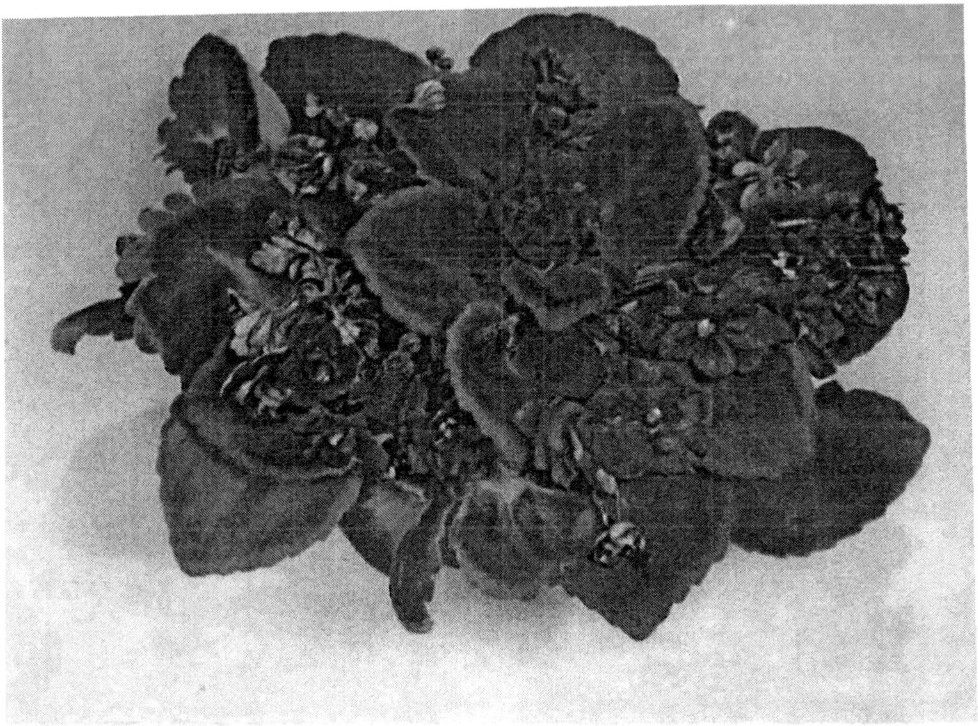

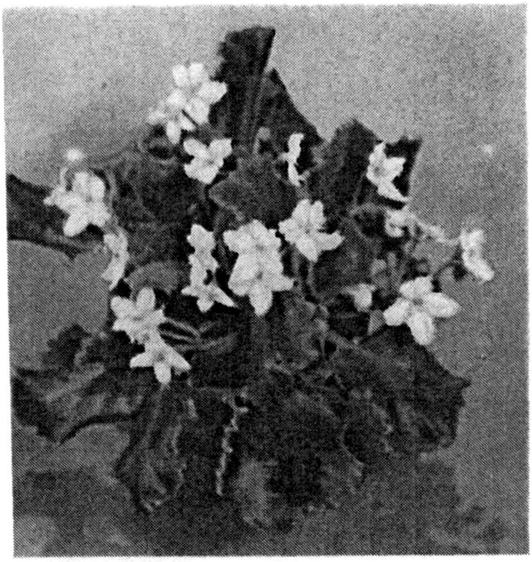

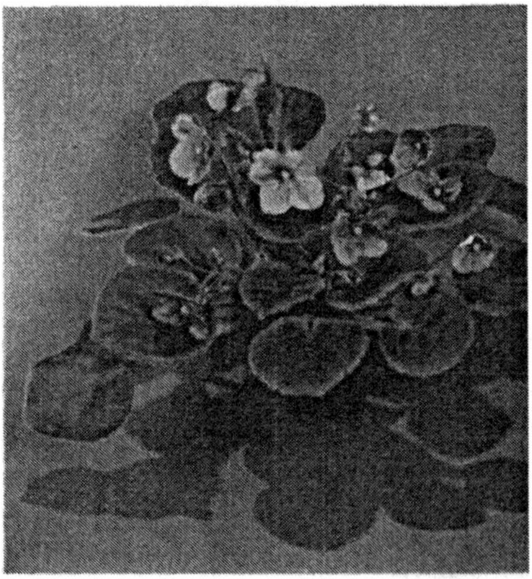

Helen Wilson

White Fringette

Tinari's America

EVIL ELEMENTS—PEST AND DISEASE

This could easily happen, particularly in Georgia and the Deep South, where bushes may harbor mealy bug.

THRIPS

Symptoms: On the leaves, a number of whitish spots appear, also blotches and dead areas along the edges. There may be wilting, even falling. Perhaps some small reddish specks will be visible. On blooms you may see white streaks, particularly noticeable on darker varieties. There will be malformations and premature bud and bloom fall. If you remove and pull apart a few flowers (not just one), you may see tiny swift-moving insects. Some fallen flowers may show a pin point opening in the anthers. Flick a few of these, and you can watch the culprits emerge.

Diagnosis: Consider all the factors. Bud and bloom drop may result from low humidity, gas in the atmosphere, or too little fresh air. Leaf blotching may also occur from a number of causes, but add petal streaking to these (don't judge on streaking alone which can be a normal reaction to radical seasonal changes, especially in autumn), and the answer probably is thrips.

If you can hold a hand lens over one of these small active pests long enough to examine it, you will see that it is gray, brown, or black, with two pairs of wings fringed with hairs. In all it is about as "thick as a thin needle and as long as a hyphen." Rasping-sucking mouth parts do the damage. Thrips scrape away surface tissues so as to dine upon the juices of leaf or flower. The dead walls of the broken cells first turn white, then rusty, as deterioration spreads from small to larger areas. The reddish specks you see, which later turn black, are excrement.

Where do thrips come from? It is hard to say but very likely from cut flowers or other plants such as the amaryllis, gladiolus, or gloxinia, or from an infested African violet added to your collection.

What to Do: One easy clean-up method is by means of Soilene. For plants in 2's and 3's sprinkle ½ teaspoon on the top of the soil in each pot and another ½ teaspoon in the saucer in which the pot sets. For plants in 5's allow a little more. Water from the top so the Soilene soaks through the soil. One treatment usually suffices. (This is also recommended for springtails.) Or dip the plant in a solution of Optox or NNOR at the rate of ½ teaspoon to 1 quart of warm water. Let the solution drip down on the soil to catch any young ones which may be there. Shade the plant for 3 days and be on the watch. Pinching off buds and flowers—if you can bear to do it—is an heroic measure. This with NNOR or Optox spraying will get rid of a multitude of thrips, when you don't want to engage in drastic dipping.

Prevention: Use soil fumigated according to the manufacturer's directions with Shell DD (chloropin), Larvacide or Dowfume G (one of the methyl bromides) or use soil which you have bought already treated; have a regular and thorough spray program to deter the enemy (and be sure to reach the top soil so as to catch the nymphs); and isolate newcomers till you are sure they are in health.

EVIL ELEMENTS—PEST AND DISEASE

MINOR PESTS

Apparently black flies are only unsightly, not harmful. Paint the pots of affected plants with liquid Pestroy or dust the plants with Pestroy or with Endopest. The flies will die.

Quarter-inch long worms, often found in organic matter, are sometimes washed out of pots after heavy watering. They are harmless. Soilene will eradicate them.

Unsightly, apparently not harmful, "springtails" are narrow white insects which appear in soil and swarm out of drainage holes when plants are watered. Soilene scattered on soil and in saucer will destroy them, or 10 percent DDT powder or Pestroy. Or you can try one enthusiast's prescription and water with Clorox solution, 1 teaspoon to 1 quart of *warm* water.

For red spider, which makes plants look gray and sickly and leaves small webs under the leaves, spray with NNOR, and do a thorough job.

CROWN ROT

Symptoms: A previously healthy plant flops, the long outer leaves drooping over the edge of the pot. Watering will not revive it, though it appears to be simply wilted. Actually it may be suffering from overwatering, particularly if the condition develops in the fall or spring. Or the sections of a plant you have just divided may go limp. Again watering will not arrest the decline.

Diagnosis: This may be crown rot, perhaps due to irregular care, resulting in "desert to swamp conditions," under which unfriendly fungous organisms thrive. These are present in most fertile soils, but are controlled by good culture. In the case of division, the fungus enters at an area of bruised or cut tissue.

What to Do: Try to reroot your plant. Remove it from the pot, shake off the soil, and do a thorough pruning job. Remove any dead roots or soft stem. Cut right back to firm healthy, green tissue, even if you must sacrifice a lot of growth. Paint the cut areas with sulphur or Fermate. Then plant the remains in peat and vermiculite, sand, or soil, or support the top so that the base reaches a steady supply of water, as in a tapered-necked vase. Unless the crown rot was caused by nematodes, your plant will probably survive. (If it starts to grow and then flops, you may safely diagnose nematodes, and had better destroy the plant.)

Prevention: Be regular in care and mindful of overwatering, and also of too deep planting. Simple crown rot is easily avoided. Avoid letting water or spray material seep down and settle in the crown of a plant. If you water from below or through a V-shaped hole in the soil, you will lessen danger. When dividing plants, or when cutting them back for rerooting, take the precaution of applying to all cut areas sulphur or Fermate. Also grow divisions on the dry side until they take hold.

PETIOLE ROT OR "EFFLORESCENCE DISEASE"

Symptoms: Leaf stalks particularly of older leaves become jellylike where they droop over and touch the sides of the pot.

You may find an orange-brown or rust-colored lesion at the point where the petiole touches the pot rim or lies in contact with soil. Some stalks may already have shriveled and collapsed. (This petiole rot is not to be confused with the normal discarding by a plant of its oldest, most mature leaves. With these there is a *gradual* yellowing and withering, actually a ripening.)

Diagnosis: Petiole or leaf-stalk rot is a chemical injury, which has been called Efflorescence Disease by Dr. Freeman Weiss. It is apparently caused by contact of leaf stalks with fertilizer salts which collect on the surface of the soil and on the rim of the pot.

Cure: Get rid of the incrustation as quickly as possible. Flush the soil with heavy waterings, about 3 times in 1 hour will do it. Stir the top soil slightly with a fork. Thereafter for a few weeks use country rain water, boiled water that has been cooled, or distilled water. Wipe any crusty residue from the pot with a damp cloth. Remove any affected leaves, cutting as far down on the stem as you can.

Prevention: Good culture will minimize this trouble by keeping petioles sturdy and so, in most varieties, held *above* pot rims. Top watering will also keep fertilizer salts flushed down into the soil where they belong. (The V-shaped hole in the soil for occasional or regular top watering is an excellent device.) Sometimes chemicals are not from fertilizer but from heavily-treated city water. If you live where this condition exists, let water stand uncovered for 24 hours before using, or boil it for 15 minutes, and then cool it. Avoid overuse of fertilizer, particularly from below. Be watchful of any damaged petioles especially on plants in plastic or glass pots on which no warning encrustation will appear. Paint any damaged areas with Fermate.

You can also provide a "barrier" between leaf and soil surface or pot rim. You can use pipe cleaners arched and inserted near the edge of the pot to look like an old-fashioned painted iron fence. Or you can put a fold of metal foil over the pot rim, or collar each plant with a paper doily, dipped in paraffin, if you expect it to last. Most popular is the method now used in some hobby greenhouses. Before planting, dip the rims of clean, dry pots one-quarter inch deep into a coffee tin of hot paraffin. With this treatment of pots, petioles seldom decay. I don't feel, however, that any such artificial arrangement should be necessary. Avoid letting fertilizer salts collect, and you can save yourself a lot of trouble.

RING SPOT

Symptoms: Yellow rings of more or less regular outline appear on the upper surfaces of the leaf.

Diagnosis: This is ring spot, one of the most easily avoided ailments, although it took considerable research to reveal that it was usually caused by the touching of soil or foliage with water or spray of a temperature varying more than 5 degrees from that of the room in which the saintpaulias were growing. Sunlight on wet foliage also causes ring spot.

Cure and Prevention: Use only room-temperature or lukewarm water or spray. When spraying, it is better to have a solution almost hot since it cools considerably in passing through the air. Keep plants away from sunlight after syringing leaves to free them of dust, or spraying in pursuit of insects.

BRIEF GUIDANCE ON PEST AND DISEASE

1. Use only sterilized soil to avoid nematodes.
2. Selenate soil to avoid mite.
3. Use an all-purpose spray or dust about once a month to guard against other troubles.
4. Practice good culture: don't overfeed, or overwater, or give too little light.

CHAPTER SEVEN

Are You a Joiner?

*All your strength is in your union,
All your danger is in discord.*
WILLIAM WADSWORTH LONGFELLOW

Half the fun of growing saintpaulias is knowing the other people who grow them too. And there are lots of them. Perhaps right in your town you have noticed ten or twelve houses with African violets in the windows. Certainly your neighbor grows them. She lives next door to you, doesn't she? No plant so easily started from a leaf ever stays in one house. In fact, in a small community where people know each other, you can almost see the pretty epidemic spread, as plants from gift leaves come to flowering size in one window after another.

If there is no club of saintpaulia enthusiasts in your town, why don't *you* start one? Everything worth while starts with some one person's enthusiastic efforts. Before 1946 there wasn't a national society either, but there were plenty of fascinated people wanting to know more about their favorite houseplant, and they turned out to be real joiners too. The African Violet Society of America, Inc. numbers more than 6000 members today, and it has held national conventions twice in Atlanta, once in Cleveland, Philadelphia, and Dayton. It was formed in Atlanta, Georgia, in the autumn of 1946 at the time the H. G. Hastings Company sponsored the first show.

THE FIRST SHOW

When plans were made the Company was aware of a certain interest in the saintpaulia, but was it surprised at what happened to the little fall exhibit that was arranged for the showroom by Charles J. Hudson, Jr.! Afterwards Mr. Hudson wrote about it:

"The traffic jam in front of the Hastings store rated newspaper headlines, and reports in the press told how extra policemen had to be assigned to keep the crowd orderly before the show opened. In a word, African violets took Atlanta by storm!

"Considering publicity and promotion, it was by far the greatest, in point of interest and attendance, of any similar show ever staged in the South. There was also the greatest interest in club promotion ever seen in the Atlanta area, there being two African violet societies formed on the evening of November 8.

"To get down to statistics, 203 persons exhibited 478 individual plants in the show. About 1,500 people were expected to view the exhibition. . . . A very conservative estimate, however, was that 8,000 people attended over the two days. Visitors came from 103 cities and towns in 14 states—Georgia, South Carolina, North Carolina, Virginia, Alabama, Tennessee, Florida, Michigan, Iowa, Maryland, Pennsylvania, Ohio, Indiana and Texas. Exhibits came from five states—Georgia, Tennessee, Alabama, South Carolina and North Carolina.

"Among the many letters—from 29 states—asking for particulars about the show, there were a number inquiring if the rumored yellow African violet would be on display. Apparently hundreds of growers had heard of this elusive color but no one had ever seen it. As a matter of fact, however, there is no such color as yellow in the genus saintpaulia. The varieties exhibited at the show, 32 of them, included Blue Boy, Blue Boy Improved, Commander, Mentor Boy, Neptune, Sailor Boy, Blue Bird, Blue Girl, Topaz Sapphire, Blue and White, Ionantha, Ionantha Grandiflora, Norseman, Amethyst, Lavender Lady, Blue Eyes, Pink Beauty, DuPont Pink, White Lady, Orchid Beauty, Trilby, Plum Pink, Mary Wac, Orchid Lady, Bicolor, Red Bicolor, Red Head, DuPont Blue, Dwarf Orchid, S-22 Bicolor, Blushing Lady, Pink Lady, Blush Beauty and a variety listed as Variegated Leaf Sport."

THE FIRST NATIONAL SOCIETY

The National Society, formed on the afternoon of November 8, 1946, elected Ferne Kellar of Des Moines, Iowa, as the first president. She had been growing violets for twenty years and knew just about all there was to know about them at that time. Alma Wright of Tennessee, Myrtle Radtke of Ohio, and Floyd L. Johnson of New York have been subsequent presidents.

Plans were made at the Hastings exhibit for a national meeting the following year. This took place in Atlanta, on October 9, 1947, with over 300 members and guests in attendance.

At once a start was made toward solving the problem of nomenclature. The Society is still working on that problem and coping with its intricacies little by little. A system of registration has now been set up with a view to having testing centers in the not-too-distant future. All you have to do is to look at the literature on the variety Orchid Beauty, to know what was attempted—and achieved. In 1947 that plant was being grown all over the country, but hardly ever by the same name. A tireless committee tracked down the fact that Betty Joe, Dark Plum, Mary Wac, Orchid Queen, Orchid Red, Plum, Plum Pink, Plum Vivid, Rosy Blue, Trilby, and Vivid Plum were one and the same—and that's but one example of what's in a name, at least in a saintpaulia name.

Beside its steady work on nomenclature, the Society is supporting one research fellowship at Ohio State University, and several others elsewhere, for the purpose of finding out more about culture; it is working on saintpaulia projects for veterans; and publishing a quarterly, *The African Violet Magazine,* which you will enjoy to the last dotted i and crossed t. I find it fascinating, and never miss a word. Here are all the answers on pests, diseases, symptoms, cures, and varieties, at least all the answers there are. Some saintpaulia questions don't have answers yet—but they will.

Most beginners read first in each issue the Homing Pigeon, a department which Elsie Freed started in 1947. It's an exchange, you know, like the old lovelorn columns, only these exchanges are about violets, and round-robin letters are circulated by groups of members. The Department is full of information, and full of people, how they manage their violets, and sometimes also how they manage their husbands, particularly any anti-saintpaulia ones who personally want more room.

There are two ways to join the African Violet Society of America, Inc. You can request membership directly from the Secretary, Mrs. Earl Mutchner, 606 Richmond Avenue, Richmond, Indiana, and enclose your $3.00 dues. You will then receive the very next issue of *The African Violet Magazine*, which is one of the wonderful privileges included in membership. As a member, you can join one of the Pigeons, which exchange leaves, as well as letters. Or you can become part of the Society through your local club, which then retains 50 cents of your membership for its own use, sending the remaining $2.50 on to the national organization. Your African violets will mean twice as much to you once you have a share in the Society.

HOW TO FORM A CLUB

So many local clubs have been formed that there's a wealth of experience at hand to guide you with yours. Why not start by making a list of possible members? Invite them to your house for a cup of tea some afternoon, or if you know that a number of men are interested, make it an evening meeting with a friendly hour or so complete with refreshments. Write about your plans to *The African Violet Magazine* (Box 1326, Knoxville, Tennessee), and ask for their free literature: (1) copies of their small information leaflets, (2) sample copies of the *Magazine*, and (3) membership applications for the approximate number you expect.

Set the time and place—your home, the home of a friend with a particularly good saintpaulia collection, or if it looks like a crowd, a club room. Do some invitation telephoning, but follow up with a card as a reminder of place, date, hour, and purpose of meeting. It's nice to have people show up on the right day!

FIRST MEETING

Keep it informal. You are planning a friendly club with a friendly purpose. No use getting excited about *Robert's Rules of Order*—at this point, anyway. Get someone to help with introductions, if prospective members aren't likely to know each other. Have a Greeter at the door who can break the ice before it forms.

From those present, select temporary officers—president, vice president, secretary, and treasurer to serve until permanent officers can be elected. Invite someone who can tell about the benefits to be derived from joining forces, and also the opportunities for fun and knowledge in the National Society. Maybe an already affiliated neighboring club will send one of its officers to your first meeting to tell ALL.

It will be a good idea to appoint some committees right off, especially the one to draw up a constitution and by-laws. The chairman of this committee can get a sample copy of the constitution of the National Society to serve as a guide. Your group probably won't want to make any changes for awhile. You can always amend later.

Try to decide on the next meeting time, and also maybe the place of the next meeting, *before* refreshments. You can never get to it once your guests start exchanging experiences and those who need to, begin asking, "How do *you* make them bloom?"

SECOND MEETING

There is real organization to be got through at this meeting, but I think there should also be a program following the business. Perhaps you can arrange a question-and-answer Stump-the-Experts party. There are always some who know a lot, and some who are interested but know nothing. If you sense timidity and a backwardness about coming forward with some real "dumb" queries, let people write their questions on slips of paper. Collect these in a hat and let the "experts" take turns drawing and answering—if they can.

Perhaps a local florist or grower would be a good speaker for Meeting Number Two. Perhaps your local garden club will have an experienced saintpaulia fan to lend you for the evening. Maybe this is the occasion for a Plant or Leaf Exchange. Later you might have a Clinic. Let members bring their ailing loved ones for advice. However, be sure to warn everyone about the danger of contaminating healthy violets at home if they place among them the invalid just back from Clinic. That plant needs two months of isolation before entering into family life again. Maybe Blue Boy left home suffering with nothing but lack of humidity, but returned with a touch of mite!

Here is a list of essential business for the chairman to try to get through at this second meeting:

1. Choose a name.
2. Decide on regular time and place of meetings. If not possible, at least settle on time and place of next meeting.
3. Adopt a constitution and by-laws, if that committee is ready to make a report.

4. Appoint a nominating committee of three.

5. Appoint other committees: *Membership.* Those who attended the first meeting should be put down as Charter Members, if they turn out to be joiners. Plans should be made to invite all others of the community who might be interested. *Reception.* A host and hostess group to make newcomers feel welcome. *Program.* Most important, for by this committee interest waxes or wanes, and the new club lives or dies. This group is responsible for securing speakers, transporting them, and making them welcome. (It should also plainly tell each one how much time is allowed for speaking. Watch out for those who just run on and on.) *Publicity.* Works right along with Program Committee. *Refreshment.* Do plan to feed more than the mind. Later you may need other committees for Door Prizes, Telephoning, "Good Cheer" (to keep in touch with members who are ill), Year Book, and Library. Don't get too complex till your club gets healthily started with saintpaulias as the main theme.

6. Introduce speaker.

7. Thank the speaker orally (have secretary send a note of appreciation afterwards), and adjourn the meeting for social purposes.

If you have a door prize—maybe someone has too many violets, which can happen—have the drawing for it and the presentation before the formal adjournment for refreshment.

That does it. Now you are joined up, and both you and your violets will be the better for it. So what's next? How about a Violet Show?

CHAPTER EIGHT

Show Business and Judging

*The world's a theater, the earth a stage
Which God and Nature do with actors fill.*
THOMAS HEYWOOD

Of course "there's no business like show business," and I don't mean just in the theater. Nothing benefits a new club more than putting on a Violet Show, for almost everyone who attends wants to grow violets too. Membership rises, enthusiasm within the old membership is stimulated, and everybody starts growing better violets because everybody has found out more about them.

If your club is almost a year old, it's time to put on a first show. And that takes planning, some six months of it for an ambitious project. It also requires somebody at the top with the disposition of a saint and a very cool head indeed. So many last minute crises develop when plants are the main performers because, even with careful planning, there is only so much that can be done ahead of show day.

Furthermore, everyone can't win a blue ribbon, even if it is nice to give A for effort. We all care so terribly for our pet plants,

SHOW BUSINESS AND JUDGING

it's hard sometimes to avoid hurt feelings when our favorites don't look as good to the judge as they do to us. However, we must be good sports. Maybe ours will get the honors next time. Meanwhile why not quietly examine the blue-ribbon winner? Why not try to find out how it surpasses our entry? Sometimes judges make critical comments on plants that don't win. Such a practice is really informing, provided the judges are tactful and kindly in criticism (as we know they try to be), and we are able to accept an impersonal criticism impersonally, as it is meant. An adverse judgment indicates flaws in the *plant*, we must understand; it is not aimed at us.

Don't attempt too much at your first show, particularly if none of the membership has had much to do with flower shows before. There is still no substitute for experience. Your first show might only be a well-displayed exhibit of clearly-labeled varieties—no blue ribbons or awards given. It would still be most interesting to the average public, many of whom don't even know there are other than purple African violets. It's better to do well what you attempt and have everybody feel good about it than to try to put on an elaborate show with many classes only to discover a host of problems, which you just haven't had the experience to solve. One service your first show can render is the answering of questions. Let the best growers among you take turns at the Question Booth, where people can get the information they long for on "how to make them bloom." Those who try to answer this, of course, must have plenty of stamina!

Eventually you will want, beside the usual classifications by color, exhibits that show how to propagate from leaves, how to cross-pollinate, how to grow from seed, various methods of growing plants in water, how to pot,—and most useful of all, a Clinic to teach what various pests and diseases do to plants, and how to avoid such trouble or get rid of it.

Your Clinic might include these departments: Pharmacy (suggestions on using alcohol, dusting sulphur, Fermate, sodium selenate); Surgery (how to remove sucker growth, cut off rotted sections of crown or root, cut apart a heavily crowned plant); Potting, Watering, Ways to Increase Humidity, even How to Make Your African Violets Bloom, with exhibits of methods and plant foods.

Then you will want some artistic displays of plants in bubble bowls, aquariums, or terrariums; colorful groupings for dining or coffee tables; groups with other plants in tray or dish gardens; plants growing in high-stemmed goblets; arrangements of plants on tiered tables, step plant stands, or on Lazy Susans.

RECOMMENDED SCALE AND SCHEDULE

The African Violet Society's own Committee on Show Preparation and Judging advises the point scale, which I give, and the Classification. The Committee favors single-crown plants only, but that does not mean your club cannot add a class for multiple-crowned plants, if you wish. Commercial exhibits must of course be kept separate from amateur exhibits. Buds do not count as blooms on an exhibited plant. No plant should be entered which has not been in the owner's possession for at least 3 months, and seedlings should be grown entirely by the ex-

SHOW BUSINESS AND JUDGING

hibitor. A sweepstakes award should be given to the member winning the most blue ribbons in a show.

SCALE OF POINTS

Leaf Pattern or Form	30
(Symmetry of Plant)	
Floriferousness	25
(Quantity of Bloom according to variety)	
Condition	20
(Cultural Perfection; freedom from diseases, insects, and marred foliage)	
Size of Bloom	15
(According to variety)	
Color	10
(Color of Bloom according to variety)	

A scale of points allows exhibitors and judges to work from the same standard and secures greater uniformity in judging.

CLASSIFICATION OF SINGLE-CROWN PLANTS ACCORDING TO COLOR

Class I   Purples
  Section   1. Blue Boy
            2. Viking
            3. Blue Girl
            4. Blue Amazon
            5. Purple Beauty, etc.
            6. Any other variety not listed

Class II   Reddish Purples
  Section   7. Commodore
            8. No. 32

9. Red Bird
10. Neptune
11. Mentor Boy, etc.
12. Any other variety not listed

Class III   Light Blue
  Section 13. Tinted Lady
    14. Blue Eyes
    15. Forget-me-not
    16. Ruffles, etc.
    17. Any other variety not listed

Class IV   Blue (Medium to Dark Blue)
  Section 18. Norseman
    19. Sailor Boy
    20. S. diplotricha
    21. S. ionantha
    22. Blue Velvet, etc.
    23. Any other variety not listed

Class V   Light Orchids
  Section 24. Amethyst
    25. Bicolor
    26. West Coast Amethyst
    27. Lilac Lady
    28. Orchid Flute
    29. Any other variety not listed

Class VI   Reds and Reddish Orchids
  Section 30. Red Head
    31. Orchid Beauty (same as Trilby)
    32. Red Lands
    33. Frieda
    34. Red duPont
    35. Gorgeous
    36. DuPont Lavender Pink
    37. Any other variety not listed

Class VII Pink
   Section 38. Pink Beauty
         39. Pink Girl
         40. Blushing Maiden, etc.
         41. Any other variety not listed

Class VIII Whites
   Section 42. White Lady
         43. White King
         44. White Supreme
         45. Snow Queen
         46. White Girl, etc.

Class IX Doubles
   Section 47. Double Russian
         48. Double Orchid Beauty
         49. Double Light Blue
         50. Double Neptune, etc.

Class X Collections
   Section 51. Best collection of 3-5 named varieties
         52. Best collection of 3-5 unnamed varieties (which includes seedlings and sports)

Class XI Novelties *(such as albinos, hanging-basket or pick-a-backs, and variegateds)*

Class XII Best Single-Crown Plant *(any variety named or unnamed)*

Class XIII Violets in a Natural Setting

Class XIV Largest Plant in the Show

Class XV Novel Plantings *(such as bubble bowls, terrariums, and unusual containers)*

Class XVI Arrangements with African Violets Predominating.

SHOW PREPARATION

The President of your club appoints the Show Chairman, and together they select committee chairmen, who then get their own committees together. The Show Chairman consults with all the other chairmen and is in full charge of the show. Your show needs these committees:

1. SCHEDULE COMMITTEE makes all rules, such as time and place of show, when entries will be received and time entries close, hour show opens, time for judging to begin, time exhibitors may remove exhibits, length of time plants must be in exhibtor's possession. Your schedule should state the method of judging the club desires to be used, either competitive or merit. Competitive form of judging is preferable (if number of judges is limited). It tends to elevate the standard of your show if only one blue, one red, and one white award is given in each class or section, if your schedule is classified according to varieties. In a large show several honorable mentions may be given if entries are worthy.

Blue Ribbon	90-100 points
Red Ribbon	80-89 points
White Ribbon	70-79 points
Honorable Mention	65-69 points

Because of the many factors that influence the growth of African violets, as fertilization, light, humidity, it is impossible to say any particular variety is difficult to grow or is very rare.

2. STAGING COMMITTEE finds a suitable location for the show.

The staging chairman must be available prior to the day of the show and until the doors are open to the public. She must make all decisions concerning disposition of space, to work out the space that will be allotted for each class, leaving aisles wide enough for entries to be roped off.

The committee should have the following items available: hammer, thumbtacks, wire, screw driver, lettering pens, extra schedules, nails, cloths and rags, string, pins, cardboard and poster board, paint, Scotch tape, tags and stickers, pencils, scissors, measuring tape, brooms, etc.

In staging some special or individual exhibits or entries, the exhibitor may provide his own metal stand or card table, or luncheon or breakfast tables.

Tables with boxes upon them of uniform size used in tiers can be covered with paper or some soft material in a color that blends with all shades of green.

In a small show the properties committee may work with the staging committee. It is responsible for the club property which is stored from show to show and for the purchase of entry cards, stickers and ribbons, etc.

3. ENTRY COMMITTEE has the duty of taking care of every entry in the show, seeing that it is properly named, recorded, and placed. The scheduled classes should be divided among the members so that each is responsible for certain classes. Each entry must be recorded in a notebook as the exhibitor brings it into the show. Entries in each class should be on a separate page. Then a card is made out for each entry, which has the exhibitor's name, class, and number in the class. This card is placed on

the plant with the exhibitor's name folded up and clipped. After the judging is completed, the clip is removed so that the exhibitor's name is displayed and the ribbon or award (if any), is attached by a judges' clerk. The entry committee should see that exhibitors conform to the schedule in placing only one entry in a class, except when a class is divided by color, variety, or other classifications. All entries should be properly labeled as to variety.

4. CLASSIFICATION COMMITTEE works with the entry committee and also the schedule committee in helping to list varieties according to color. Two or three members are sufficient. They should be familiar with all varieties and able to recognize them readily. It is important that this committee know which varieties are similar and the correct names of each variety. They should also be familiar with diseases and not hesitate to disqualify suspicious plants for the protection of other exhibitors. They give advice to the entries committee as to the proper classes in which to enter exhibits. If the judges detect what they believe to be an error, they must call it to the attention of the classification committee to correct.

5. PUBLICITY COMMITTEE builds up public interest through posters, radio announcements, and newspaper articles. A detailed account of your show, stressing outstanding exhibits, names of judges and names of all prize winners in all classes should be given to the newspaper after the judging. Newspaper photographers may be invited to attend. A large placard with the scale of points (fully explained as to what each one includes)

SHOW BUSINESS AND JUDGING

may be placed where visitors may see how the judges made their decisions.

6. CHAIRMAN OF JUDGES secures judges, sends them schedules, arranges transportation. The names of judges should be withheld from the public until after the show. Judges should never enter the exhibition room until the show is completely ready.

Usually three judges suffice for the average show. If a large show is held, two groups of judges may be used, each group judging certain classes.

As to entertaining your judges, that is up to the judging committee. They are usually met at the train, bus, or airport, if they travel in any of those ways. They may be served a light refreshment before judging, then lunch after judging is completed. The judges' transportation, meals, and hotel (if necessary) should be paid by the club. It is also the duty of the chairman of judges to write a note of thanks to each judge.

7. THE JUDGES' CLERKS serve as attendants to the judges. They should be instructed in their duties and know the rules of the schedule governing the show. Two clerks are recommended to each group of judges, one to record the awards in the entry book, and one to place ribbons or seals on the exhibits. They should be equipped with entry books, ribbons, stickers, pencils, erasers, and extra schedules. Clerks should never volunteer information. They may answer any question, secure needed information, and run errands. They should keep far enough away from the judges to allow them to talk freely.

The clerk may also write the judges' comments in the entry book or on a card to be placed with the exhibit, if asked to do so by the judges. No one but judges, clerks, and the chairman of judges or general show chairman should be present while the show is being judged.

After judging is completed, the clerks should compile a list of prize-winning exhibits for the club's record and for the publicity chairman.

8. Hospitality Committee acts as hostess, greets visitors, answers questions, tries to see that plants are not handled.

ABOUT JUDGES

Besides being a monument of fairness, courage, and tact, the good judge needs to have above all a thorough knowledge of varieties, know signs of health and illness so she can wisely eliminate any infested or diseased entries, and understand the effects of exposures, fertilization, humidity, watering, etc. However, if you are putting on a little show with local judges, don't expect such a Solomon. Pick people who grow violets and let them do the best they can. Shows are supposed to be fun, not just exercises in character development. Above all stand by your judges and let it be known that their decisions must be final. If you would rather have an outside judge, write to The African Violet Society of America, Inc. and ask them for suggestions of qualified judges near your town.

Judges can be trained. The Society is organizing schools throughout the country to qualify members as apprentice judges.

SHOW BUSINESS AND JUDGING

On occasion the Society puts on a Judging School at the time of the annual convention. At two sessions all aspects of judging are discussed, examinations given, and certificates bestowed.

African violets being special plants require special judging so that the holder of a judge's certificate from the National Council of State Garden Clubs is unlikely to be qualified, unless to her knowledge of garden plants she also adds knowledge of saintpaulias. If she has this, her experience in judging will be valuable, since the same techniques apply to all flower judging. Incidentally, particularly in small clubs, judges should not be disqualified from exhibiting. They should simply bow out to another room while the class in which they are represented is judged by others.

ENTRY CARDS

The National Society uses this type of card for its show business.

```
Section I
Class 3
Entry No. 7
_____(marked here to fold up)
Name   Miss A. V. Smith
```

The exhibitor's name is folded over and fastened with a paper clip until the judging is finished. Then it may be unfolded and displayed so that congratulations may be personally received—and enjoyed—by the winners.

SHOW TERMS

Amateur Grower. One who grows plants for pleasure, not to sell.

Commercial Grower. One who buys, grows, sells, and advertises plants, as a business enterprise.

Disqualify. To remove an entry, which cannot be considered by the judges, because it does not conform to schedule, as a multiple-crowned plant in a class calling for singles. The reason for disqualifying is written on the entry card.

Eliminate. To remove an entry, which cannot be considered by the judges, because it has no chance of award, as a diseased, lopsided, or generally poor specimen.

Entry. Single plant or unit entered in accordance with the schedule's requirements.

Exhibit. Plant or plants on display but not in competition.

HINTS ON GROOMING

Since *symmetry* counts for a big 30 points and can be developed only over a long growing period, better start to train your plant in the way it should go, the minute your seedling is put into its first pot. Set it firmly in the center and remember the daily quarter turn (clockwise) at the window so growth will be even—and characteristic. That's the important thing. The upright Amethyst, Bicolor, and Blue Eyes are not supposed to develop the flat tight rosette of Commodore or Frieda, nor the droopy growth of duPont Lavender Pink or Dainty Maid. Show plants should give full evidence of their nature.

SHOW BUSINESS AND JUDGING

If an important leaf in the lowest circle of leaves gets broken off and leaves a gap like the opening in a six-year-old's teeth, you will have to train the leaves on each side of the gap to cover it up. Let hairpins, strong ones, or toothpicks come to the rescue. Insert them on the outside of the leaves you wish to close in, and each day move them so as to make the gap narrower. Eventually the leaves will take the hint and grow where you have firmly indicated they should.

Train to a regular outline. Sometimes one leaf grows out beyond all others. You will have to take such a one off, and train the others to cover up. Irregular plants may be more interesting and perhaps prettier in the window, but show business is different, and in a way, artificial.

Don't worry if one of your Supremes or Amazons has only a few flowers at show time. It will be judged on *quantity of bloom* (25 points) comparatively with other Supremes and Amazons, not against Blue Boy.

The same holds for *size of bloom* (15 points). A duPont Blue Hybrid is expected to have almost 3-inch flowers, but Sailor Boy only 1½-inch blooms.

Variability in color (10 points) is expected by all good judges who are familiar with the change of color wrought in saintpaulias by differences in soil, water, and exposure.

Cultural Condition (20 points) should be just about perfect, no leaves bleached by sun, no imperfect foliage, no spots, no insects, no disease traces, no dead bloom stalks. Neither size, nor multitude of bloom can help a plant that looks culturally seedy and not absolutely in the pink.

LITTLE THINGS THAT COUNT

Do have pots well scrubbed. Clean containers contribute so much to a spruced-up look.

Label plants, as to variety, so the public knows what it's looking at. Nothing irritates me—and everyone else—more at a flower show than to see something I really want, that's rare perhaps, and not be able to find a soul to tell me what it is. The man who knows is always "out to lunch."

Label plants also as to ownership. Write your name with pencil, which won't blur like ink if it gets wet, on a piece of adhesive and fasten it to the bottom of the pot. Then there won't be any question which Blue Girl belongs to you.

Water your plants well so they won't get droopy if the exhibition room gets warm.

Syringe them well near show time to remove all dust, but don't let this be a day-before job because a few blooms almost always get knocked off in syringing.

And since your show plant is your treasure, be sure it gets a thorough spraying right after the show, just in case it picked up something it shouldn't have.

Well, now it's over you are feeling it was a pretty big undertaking, putting on a show. But wasn't it worth while, wasn't it fun? And aren't you popping with ideas for a bigger and better show next year? Of course!

CHAPTER NINE

Wrap It Up

> Precious things deserve a covering fair,
> Inside and out, both need, the owner's care.
> NADINA CARSON

Every saintpaulia fancier needs to know how to wrap leaves, and sometimes plants too, for safe mailing or shipping. There will always be specimens at your window that can spare a few leaves to add new varieties to someone else's collection. There will always be occasions when, from your own abundance, you will want to select a plant for a distant friend's birthday or Christmas present. So I am outlining here the methods used by growers to mail leaves and ship plants. You can interpret their materials practically into what you have to hand.

PATENTED PLANTS

You know that some varieties are protected by a government patent. Among them are Blue Girl, White Lady, Pink Beauty, Lady Geneva, Gorgeous, and Pink Girl. Legally you may not propagate these varieties vegetatively without permission. You may however, use their pollen in breeding without infringing on the patent rights.

The purpose of the patent is to insure some return on the long investment of time and money, which is behind every origination. Unfortunately patenting plants does not work too well. A plant patent is meant to serve the horticultural scientist as a patent on a radio protects the inventor. The Plant Patent Law was passed in 1930. If you find those small sticks a nuisance, keep in mind how much such protection means to men who give their lives to producing better plants for you and me. Luther Burbank, the great plant breeder who was responsible for some of the finest fruits we enjoy today, once said, "A man can patent a mousetrap or copyright a nasty song, but if he gives to the world a new fruit, he will be fortunate if he is rewarded by so much as having his name connected with the results."

If you are a *commercial grower* and wish to handle the patented varieties, you may obtain a propagating license by applying to the following firms: to Ulery Greenhouses, 1325 Maiden Lane, Springfield, Ohio, for Blue Girl; to Fred C. Gloeckner and Company, Inc., 15 East 26th Street, New York 10, New York, for White Lady; and to Holton and Hunkel Company, 797 N. Milwaukee Street, Milwaukee 1, Wisconsin, for Pink Beauty; to R. G. Baxter, Box 1444, Youngstown, Ohio, for Gorgeous and Pink Girl; and to Geneva and Sunnydale Nurseries, 250 Sherwin Street, San Francisco, California, for Lady Geneva.

Permission involves the signing of a contract with the owners and arrangements to buy plant sticks at a stated fee, usually

$2.50 per hundred. These sticks bear the name of the plant and its patent number. You are required to place a label on every plant or leaf you sell, or give away, of a patented variety. Whether you stand the approximate cost of 2½ cents per stick, or your customer does, is entirely up to you.

SOME SUBSTITUTE VARIETIES

Every complete collection should include one each of the lovely patented varieties, but if your space is rather limited and you do not wish to become involved in propagating these, there are substitutes for the color range. Of course, there are no available duplicates for the same combinations of flower and foliage. Here are some possibilities.

For Blue Girl: Purple Girl, Emperor Wilhelm, and with the same girl-type foliage but with other flower colors—Bronze Girl, Light Blue Girl, Mulberry Girl, Red Head Girl, Sailor Girl—several of the Gypsy group, and all of the My Lady Series.

For White Lady: Eva's White, Snow Prince, Snow Queen, White Girl, White King, White Queen, White Sister, and White Waterlily.

For Pink Beauty: Pink Leatherneck, Pink Perfection, Pink Princess, Pink Star, Tinari's Pink Luster, Dainty Maid, and the paler Blushing Maiden.

For Gorgeous: Grand Lady and the smaller Red Spoon.

For Pink Girl: Gypsy Pink and Shrimpie.

For Lady Geneva there are no exact alternates, although there are many other handsome variegateds, Blue-Eyed Beauty, Lady Ulery, Star-of-Bethlehem—and more to come.

WRAPPING AND MAILING LEAVES

The inexpensive way to achieve variety is to swap leaves with other collectors or to buy leaves from growers who sell them as well as the rooted plants. You can then propagate for yourself and slowly but surely develop extensive representation. When leaves are exchanged, the aim is to pack them so that they can travel well through the mails to great distances. They should arrive in such fresh condition that full vitality remains to nourish a new crop of plants.

When preparing leaves for mailing, you will find it a good plan to wrap the entire leaf *stem* in moist sphagnum moss (the florist uses this extensively for packing), cotton, or in damp peatmoss. Enfold *the leaf itself* loosely but completely with dry excelsior, a piece of facial tissue, or again with cotton. Enclose the entire protected leaf then in a stiff layer of waxed paper.

Fasten the leaf to a section of strong corrugated paper and place the whole thing in a cardboard box. Finally wrap, tie, and label for parcel post or first-class mailing. First class is more expensive, of course, but also quicker and in this transaction speed is of the essence. The trick is to keep the leaves as short a time as possible out of a growing medium of water or soil, and in transit to maintain moist stems and dry tops. It is also important to prevent any shifting of the leaf during the journey. Wrapping must be thick enough to protect leaves from crushing in handling and particularly when the box is stamped. In warm weather holes should be punched in the heavier coverings to provide some means of ventilation.

It is also possible to mail in a container especially prepared for saintpaulias, and called a leaf-mailing kit. This is simply a thick cardboard cylinder capped with a metal-reinforced screwed-on lid. A supply of heavy cellophane envelopes and narrow labels is included to hold leaves. A piece of thin cardboard fits snugly across the center to prevent shifting.

ZONING REGULATIONS

Whether you live in a quarantined Japanese beetle zone or not does not matter when only leaves are involved. If whole plants are being mailed or shipped, they are not permitted to go out of quarantined zones into beetle-free zones except after inspection, unless every bit of soil is first washed from the roots. You can get more specific information on zoning by writing to the Bureau of Plant Quarantine, Department of Agriculture, in your own state. At the present time, I learn from the national Department of Agriculture that either the whole or part of the following states are in quarantined zones: Connecticut, Delaware, District of Columbia, Maine, Maryland, Massachusetts, New Hampshire, New Jersey, New York, Ohio, Pennsylvania, Rhode Island, Vermont, Virginia, and West Virginia.

Mailing *into* quarantined zones poses no problem. It is the outgoing carriers of the dreaded Japanese beetle pest which the government is so justifiably interested in. (See also page 110ff.)

CANADIAN IMPORTATIONS

If you live in Canada and wish to have saintpaulia leaves or plants sent to you, you must obtain a permit for the importation of this "Nursery Stock," even if in your opinion it's just a matter of a hobby exchange of leaves. Write for a permit to the Chief, Division of Plant Protection, Science Service, Department of Agriculture, Ottawa, Ontario to cover *each* importation. State clearly (1) Number of leaves or plants, (2) Kind and variety, (3) Value, (4) Name and address of importer, (5) Name and address of shipper, (6) Point of destination, if other than importer's address, (7) How shipment is to be made, i.e., first-class mail, parcel post, express, or freight.

A numbered permit will be mailed to you, along with special mailing labels for first class or parcel post deliveries. After you receive these, send (1) your order, (2) your permit number, and (3) mailing labels to the United States grower supplying you. Do not send the permit. Hold on to that until your customs office notifies you of the arrival of your order. Surrender it only when your receive clearance papers, and the stock. (And may I say I hope you won't be too exhausted to take care of the stuff once you get it.)

If you live in the United States, there is another kind of red tape for you. You proceed by the Authority of Plants and Seed Quarantine, Number 37. To *import* from Canada you write for a permit to the Import and Permit Section, Bureau of Entomology and Plant Quarantine, 209 River Street, Hoboken, New Jersey. Then the Canadian supplier must obtain a certificate of Examination and Origin from his Canadian Department of Agriculture.

To export plants to Canada, permission must be obtained from the Department of Agriculture, Science Service, Division of Plant Protection, Ottawa, Ontario.

To export leaves to Canada, you must first take the leaves for inspection to a local office of the U. S. Department of Agriculture, Bureau of Entomology and Plant Quarantine. The inspector will issue a certificate and this certificate from our State Department of Agriculture will also satisfy the Canadian Department. (And I can only hope your friend in Canada will appreciate what you have gone through for her.)

HOW TO WRAP A PLANT

Perhaps the simplest method of wrapping, for amateur grower or professional, is the one illustrated. Materials include: two pieces of waxed paper, one cut in a square and the other a sheet two feet long; brown wrapping paper, at least 16 inches wide; two widths of brown gummed tape; a corrugated board, large enough to shape into a box 4 by 4 by 12 inches; and crumpled or shredded newspaper.

The potted plant is first set on the smaller piece of waxed paper, which is gently but firmly tucked in over the edge of the pot. This serves to hold in the soil and to support the leaves in an almost upright position. The plant is next laid on its side at the narrow end of the longer piece of waxed paper. One hand then eases the leaves into a straight position; the other rolls at the girth of the pot until 4 or 5 inches of paper remains. The lower end is then folded up, the remainder is rolled and sealed with 1-inch paper tape. The loose top end may be carefully tucked in, if length of leaves permits. The resulting package should have no flare but be perfectly upright.

The second step is then repeated, using the heavy wrapping

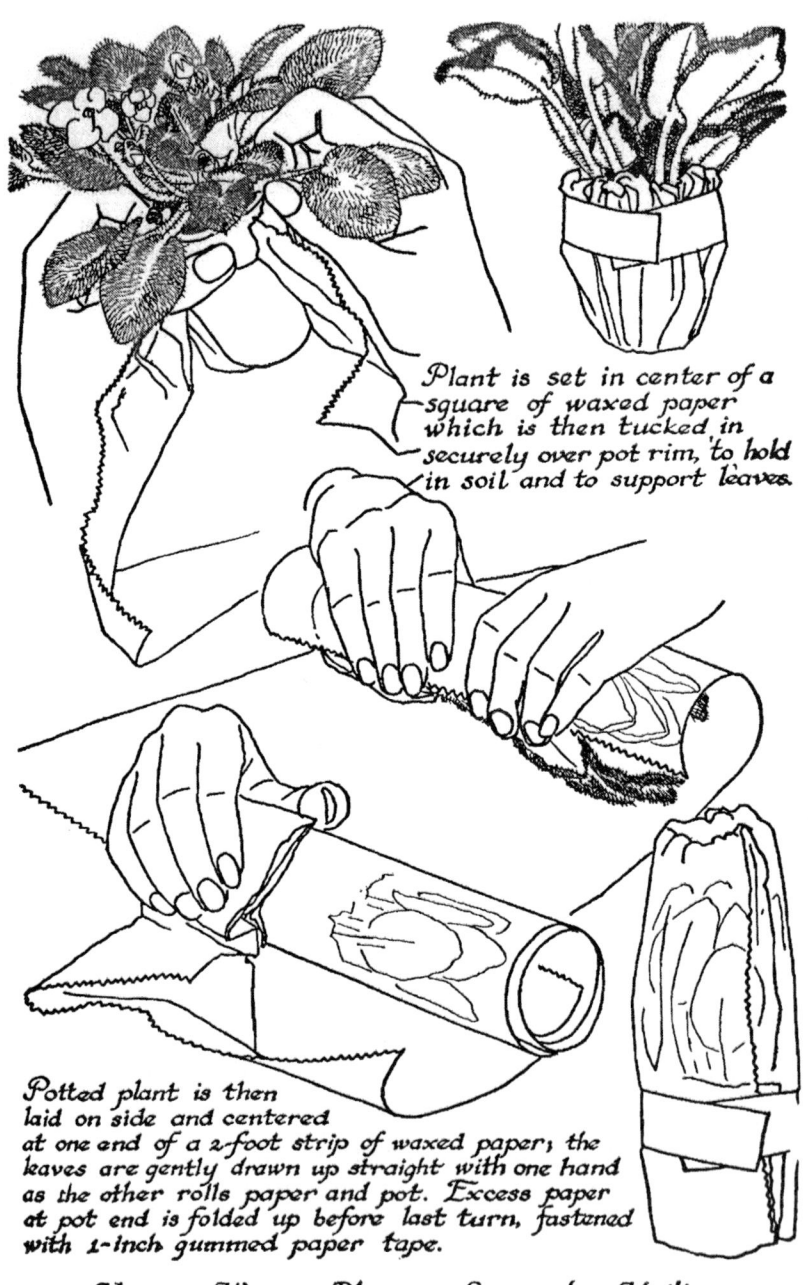

Plant is set in center of a square of waxed paper which is then tucked in securely over pot rim, to hold in soil and to support leaves.

Potted plant is then laid on side and centered at one end of a 2-foot strip of waxed paper; the leaves are gently drawn up straight with one hand as the other rolls paper and pot. Excess paper at pot end is folded up before last turn, fastened with 1-inch gummed paper tape.

How to Wrap a Plant or Leaves for Mailing

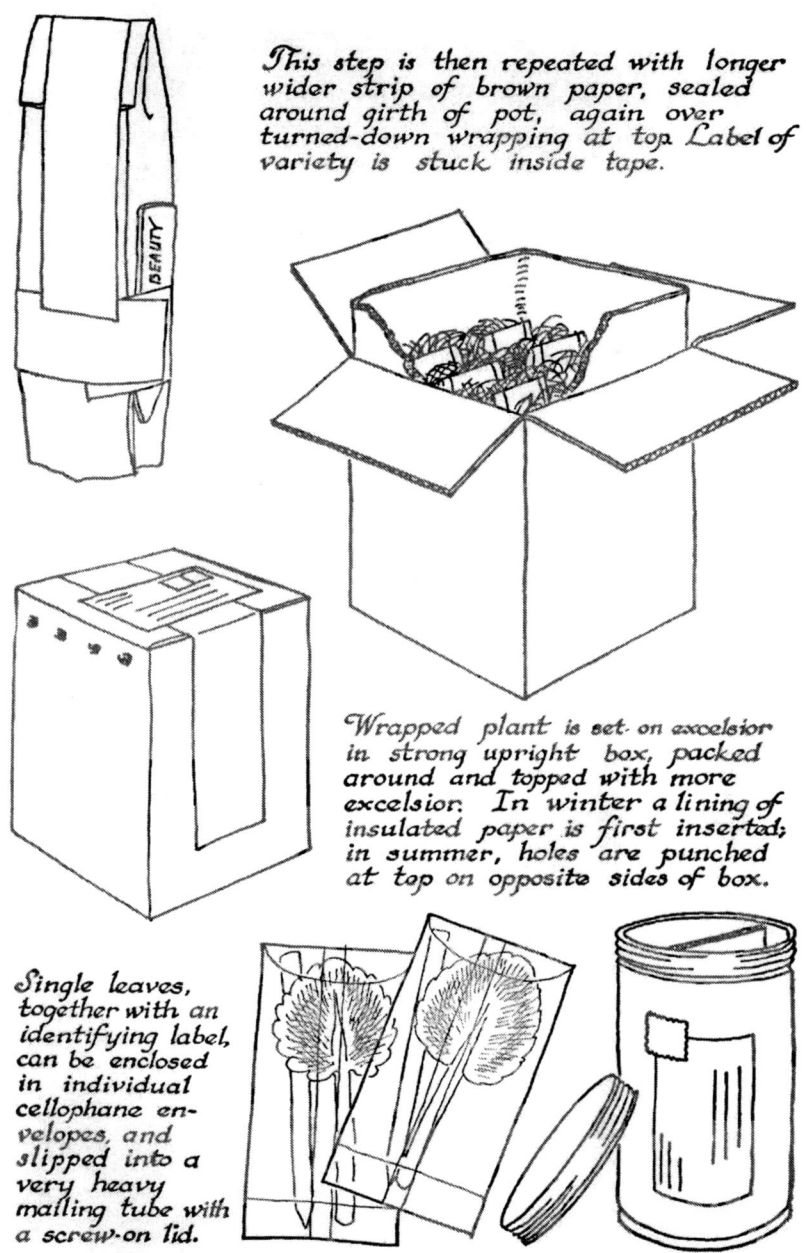

This step is then repeated with longer wider strip of brown paper, sealed around girth of pot, again over turned-down wrapping at top. Label of variety is stuck inside tape.

Wrapped plant is set on excelsior in strong upright box, packed around and topped with more excelsior. In winter a lining of insulated paper is first inserted; in summer, holes are punched at top on opposite sides of box.

Single leaves, together with an identifying label, can be enclosed in individual cellophane envelopes, and slipped into a very heavy mailing tube with a screw-on lid.

How to Wrap a Plant or Leaves for Mailing

paper. The rolled plant should be centered on it in order that enough remain at top and bottom to fold up. The label bearing the name of the variety is tucked into the tape securing this wrapping.

Finally the plant is placed on crumpled newspaper in a box of heavy corrugated board. It is packed by itself, or in an appropriately larger box, which holds 4 or 6 plants. Once a plant is packed gently but firmly in the crumpled newspaper—up to the very top—there is no possibility of shifting inside the box. In winter, a layer of insulated paper, the kind used in bags for frozen food, is wrapped around the plant after the stuffing has been completed. The box is finally sealed at the top and labeled there. In warm weather, no insulating paper is used, but for aeration a line of holes is punched along both sides. For summer mailing particularly, excelsior provides better aeration as a packing material, but the newspaper is more readily available.

CHAPTER TEN

The Species—a Fascinating History

There is no finality in the interpretation of nature.
LIBERTY HYDE BAILEY

Some fifty years ago the African violet was discovered in "the hilly regions of Eastern tropical Africa," and in 1893 it flowered for the first time in Europe, thousands of miles from its native haunts. From the day of its discovery, the saintpaulia took the horticultural world by storm. An important garden magazine of the time noted, beside the drawing we have reproduced: "It does not often happen that a plant newly introduced into Europe can claim the honor accorded to the subject of this plate, of being within two years of its flowering figured in five first-class horticultural periodicals." (See page 171.)

The African violet, East African violet, or Usambara violet, as it is also called, is of course not a violet at all, even though it does come from Africa and its more usual deep purple blooms are of violet form and color. Actually it is a member of the Gesneria family, to which belongs also the velvet-leaved gloxinias, the episcias, some of which are scarlet, and the naegelias, the probable source of a yellow violet through crossbreeding, if such is indeed a possibility.

The African violet was first discovered by Baron Walter von Saint Paul, the Imperial District Captain of Usambara, a province of North East Tanganyika in the Territory of East Africa. He sent either seeds or more likely plants of "das violette Usambara" to his father, Hofsmarschal Baron von Saint Paul of Fischbach in Silesia. The father was, fortunately for us, a man keenly interested in plants. In fact he was president of the Dendrological Society of Germany, a group devoted to the study of trees.

To the publisher of *Curtis Magazine*, that enchanting English publication, which you can perhaps find in bound volumes among the horticultural books in your library, he wrote:

"The *Saintpaulia* was discovered by my son, who lives in East Africa where he owns plantations of vanilla and India-rubber trees. It was found in two localities; one about an hour from Tanga, in wooded places, in the fissures of limestone rocks, as well as in rich soil with plenty of vegetable matter. This place is not more than fifty to one hundred and fifty feet above the sea level. The second place is in the primeval forest of Numbara, likewise in shady situations, but on granite rocks, two thousand five hundred feet above the sea. It is much more plentiful in the former place. Several varieties have been discovered that differ slightly in color of the flowers but all are blue."

The Hofsmarschal took plants to Herman Wendland, Director of the Royal Botanical Gardens at Herrenhausen. It was the Director who named the plant for the Saint Paul family, described it in Latin, and gave it the species name, ionantha, "with

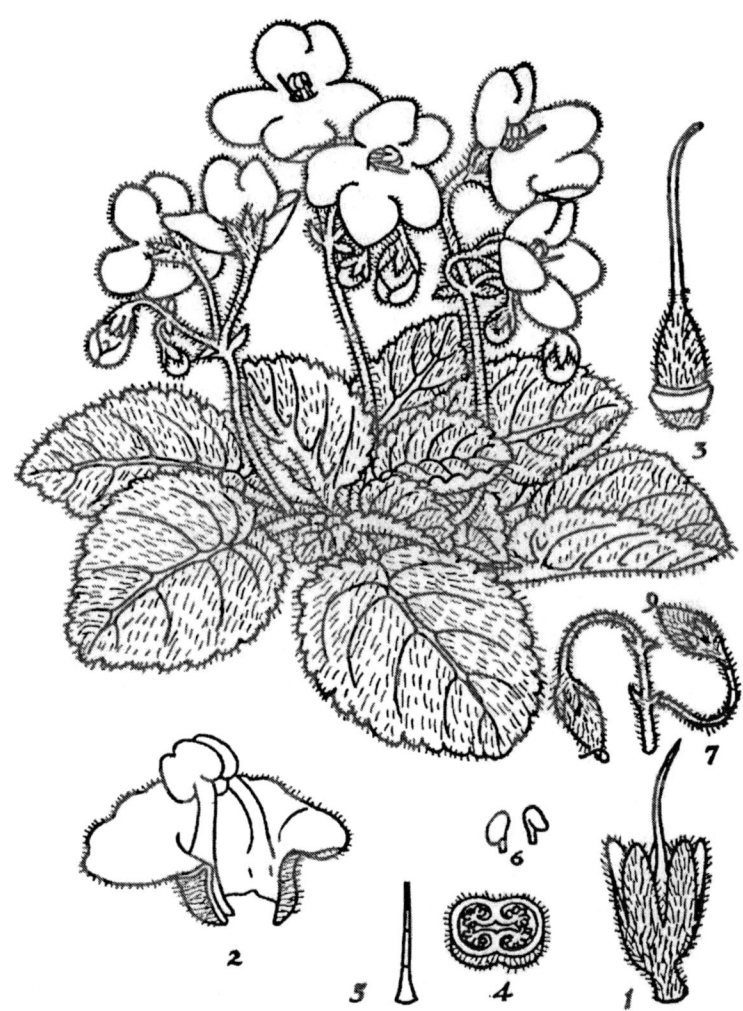

Saintpaulia ionantha. 1. calyx and style; 2. tube of corolla laid open and stamen; 3. ovary and disk; 4. transverse section of ovary; 5. hair of margin of corolla; 6. ovules; 7. immature fruit.

violet-like flowers." He exhibited flowering plants in Ghent at the International Horticultural Exhibit, where they "shared with Eulophiella exhibited by Messrs. Linden the honour of being the two most botanically interesting plants in the exhibition." The next year continental nurserymen carried the seed and the *Revue L'Horticulture Belge et Etrangere,* beside a picture of a rather unrealistic and very blue saintpaulia with very pink petal reverses, remarked *"Sa floraison est ininterrompue pendant tout d'hiver . . . Elle sera promptement accuellie par tous les amateurs auxquels elle promet les plus vives jouissances aux époque de l'année où les fleurs sont les plus rares."* And plants of this marvelous subject blooming "in the time of year when flowers are rarest" were offered by L'Etablissement Ed. Pynaert-Van Geert for six francs each. Flowering plants were also developed in the Royal Gardens of England.

The first commercial plantman to see the possibilities of our violet and offer it to the world was Friedrich Benary of the seed house of Ernst Benary of Erfurt, Germany. Evidently the firm received rights in 1893, and seed production and distribution were started. A red-violet variety was announced in 1898. Then alba, a white, and various others as atrocoerulea and purpurea. It is good to hear from Mr. Evan Roberts that this enterprising firm continues today under the management of Friedrich's son, Ernst, and a grandson. Mr. Roberts reports that, "The present Mr. Ernst Benary is now offering a dark blue, an amaranth red, and a light blue, heart-shaped variety to the trade."

At the outset Mr. Ernst Benary made certain interesting observations on the new plant he was handling, "It seems to be quite a peculiarity of this plant to produce capsules of two different shapes ... one long and the other round-shaped." He added that the different types of capsule were never found on the same plant. It is now concluded that only the short-fruited plants were specimens of S. ionantha.

In recent years Mr. B. L. Burtt of the Herbarium at Kew in England has designated the long-fruited plants as S. diplotricha. These have a "dual indumentum of long and short hairs which clothe the leaves, contrasting with the hairs of uniform length found on S. ionantha." When I talked with Mr. Burtt in England in 1949, he felt that further investigation was going to reveal a number of species. He had already noted two more. Saintpaulia tongwensis "has longer more elliptic leaves with a subacute tip; it also has longer fruits, which are densely haired. Saintpaulia orbicularis is characterized by its orbicular leaves, which are cordate at the base, and by the flowers being smaller and more numerous and of a paler color ... upper side of corolla almost pure white, but with a deep lavender ring round the anther cells, underside of lobes white with light crimson middle vein and tips washed with colors; ... All these four Species [including S. ionantha] are typically rosette plants, but there is another species, S. grotei ... which has a creeping stem rooting at the nodes."

Meanwhile in this country the investigation had been undertaken by Evan Paul Roberts of the Department of Horticulture, Michigan State College, and Harvey Cox of California. Their fascinating articles have appeared regularly since March, 1950, in the *African Violet Magazine*. All of us interested in the past of the saintpaulia, as well as its lively present and marvelously unpredictable future, have enjoyed the reports.

Indeed knowledge of the various species is of the greatest general interest. Collectors as well as breeders are therefore most grateful for the research which Evan Roberts has undertaken. We are pleased, too, that Harvey Cox is growing plants of the available species and hope that eventually there will be a good stock of them. He has some interesting hybrids coming along selected, as he says, "from a large group of seedlings having S. grotei or S. tongwensis as seed or pollen parent. They were bred and selected for desirable foliage characteristics and are outstanding in that respect. Individuals of this group vary as to size and shape of blade but all are thin bladed and wiry of petiole. I am not satisfied with the size and color of blossoms, therefore they will be used as breeding stock and continue to be known by number rather than name.

"Recent experience with a group of F 2 seedlings confirmed the belief that any color or any shape of flower can be bred to stock foliage in two generations. This batch flowered in all shades from lighter than Blushing Maiden to darker than any named pink I know. The stock foliage was what we call oak leaf in shape and darkest green in color.

"To my mind, S. grotei has two good characteristics—thin texture of blade and less succulent petioles. Saintpaulia tongwensis has a uniform habit of growth and does not sucker like so many of the varieties, and species too for that matter. The leaf of S. orbicularis is slick and shines like that of a begonia. The other newly introduced species will not in my mind contribute anything worth while to the hybridizers stock of material."

We miss so much if we are unaware of the history of our favorite plants. I discovered that in my previous study of gera-

THE SPECIES—A FASCINATING HISTORY

niums, I mean of course the true ones or pelargoniums. Until I had the full picture of their heritage, they are also African, and their "wanderings" in Holland and England, I never really *knew* them, despite years of growing.

Because the species are so important, I am sure we all feel that The African Violet Society of America, Inc. could not have bestowed a more popular honor in 1951 than their Bronze Medal Award to Evan Roberts and Harvey Cox. Now we hope they will continue to discover and report on more of the saintpaulia species—and also grow them for us.

There is considerable difference in the growth habits of the species now known. While the species of any plant are seldom as attractive as the varieties, and rarely as large-flowered, they have great value for the plant breeder. Our present violets are probably descendants of S. ionantha and S. diplotricha. A new race of creeping, cascade, or climbing saintpaulias might be developed from S. grotei, goetzeana, and magungensis, new leaf patterns are possible from S. tongwensis with its pale center banding.

A species, as you know, is a plant as nature produces it. Botanists classify plants as to family, in this case, Gesneria; genus, as Saintpaulias; species, as ionantha, diplotricha, or grotei; and variety, as Blue Boy or White Lady, to mention but two of hundreds. A name, following the species, points to the one who first described it, as E. P. Roberts after S. magungensis. All of these species have come from Tanganyika Territory in East Africa.

The species descriptions which follow are based on the excellent Roberts-Cox reports.

SAINTPAULIA AMANIENSIS E. P. ROBERTS

This species was discovered in the foothills of the Usambara Mountains near Amani and appears to be related to S. magungensis, S. grotei, and S. goetzeana, all of which have creeping stems.

The violet-blue flowers with deeper centers appear in pairs, and measure about 2.7 cm. across. The leaves are medium green above, pale greenish white below, ovate to ovate-elliptical, 2.5-5 cm. long and 2-3.5 cm. wide. Margins are "crenate-dentate, slightly revolute" with midrib prominent. Petioles are 4-9 cm. long, "stems procumbent branched, rooting where they come in contact with soil, pale green, up to 10 cm. long." Vegetative parts are covered with long and short hairs intermixed. (Saintpaulia amaniensis differs from S. magungensis in having oval pointed, rather than rounded leaves.)

SAINTPAULIA DIPLOTRICHA B. L. BURTT

This species was found on November 26, 1895, at altitudes of 1000 to 3000 feet on gneiss rock in the region of sacred Mt. Mlinga. The locale is fifteen miles north of Mt. Tongwe, the home of S. tongwensis, in the East Usambara Mountains. The situation has a moister atmosphere than that of tongwensis, and, in cultivation, diplotricha has shown need for more water. This is the other of those two species which Ernst Benary grew but did not distinguish, except to note that his plants bore different kinds of seed capsules. We know the round ones belonged to ionantha, the long type to diplotricha, which was previously and

S. diplotricha, Species

erroneously identified as kewensis. (Today no plant bears the name kewensis.)

Saintpaulia diplotricha, so called for its covering of two kinds of hairs, blooms prolifically, producing clusters of 2 or 3 deep violet flowers, 1-inch across, and well above the foliage. The leaf is medium to light green, quite thin with slightly serrate margins, very smooth, slightly quilted, flat, and measuring 1⅝ to 2 inches. The petiole is thin, about 2 inches long.

The plants described by the African Violet Society in their first records were almost miniature, flat, of light rosette growth. Our drawing shows such a dwarf grower. This was easily propagated and tended to sucker freely. It now appears that if allowed to produce multiple crowns, diplotricha will develop into a very large plant.

SAINTPAULIA GOETZEANA ENGLER

This species was found by W. Goetze on large boulders among moss in the primeval forest of the central part of Uluguru on the south side of the Lukwangule plateaus. The discoverer sent a good herbarium specimen to Professor Adolph Engler in Berlin, who published a description of it in his *Botanische Jahrbücher* on July 13, 1900. To date no specimens have been introduced into the United States. The Engler description does not mention color, but we are led to presume it is much the same as that of S. ionantha. The drawing shows a rounded leaf, "1.8-2.8 cm. long and wide" and clusters of 3 flower stems with buds and blossoms. The flower stem is 3-3.5 cm. long. There is the same creeping stem as in grotei and magungensis.

SAINTPAULIA GROTEI ENGLER

This species has been found "in the vicinity of Amani, Tanganyika Territory, at an altitude of 3000 feet . . . in dense shade near running water . . . roots are not submerged but located where drainage is perfect." Grotei was first described in 1921 by Professor A. Engler of Berlin. Present-day plants, with benefit of greenhouse, produce larger flowers than those of the Professor's description.

The flowers, in clusters of 2 or 3, are blue violet near the tips of the petals, shading darker toward the center (BV.5 to BV.2). Seed pods measure over an inch. The rounded, dentate leaf is medium green, almost flat, measuring 1 to 3½ inches. Sometimes small pockets or depressions appear between veins. The long, brown, leaf stems are the most obvious characteristic of grotei. On occasion these produce roots at the nodes, those small swellings you see on the stems.

The long stems make it possible for anyone to develop with grotei a cascade, hanging, or climbing plant, if a support is provided. The plant breeder will discover in grotei all kinds of stimulating possibilities.

SAINTPAULIA IONANTHA H. WENDLAND

This was one of the two species, but not recognized as two, discovered by Baron von Saint Paul in Tanga at 100 to 150 feet above sea level. To date it is the only species we know which grows at so low an altitude. Saintpaulia ionantha and S. diplotricha appear to be the ancestors of the hundreds of present-day

S. ionantha, Species (Modern)

varieties. Our drawing of S. ionantha from *Curtis Magazine* looks much like the ionantha we know today. (See page 171.)

Saintpaulia ionantha produces light blue-violet clusters of 3 to 8 flowers, each about 1½ inches in diameter. The leaves are dark green, glossy, quilted with slightly serrated margins and cordate bases. Leaves cup upward slightly and measure 2½ by 3½ inches. Petioles are sometimes flushed red, and grow up to 7 inches long. The plant is a very large, upright grower with somewhat drooping lower leaves. The heat tolerance of today's varieties is doubtless due to ionantha inheritance, since the average temperature of Tanga is 80 degrees F.

SAINTPAULIA MAGUNGENSIS E. P. ROBERTS

This new species, first described by Mr. Roberts in the *African Violet Magazine* for June, 1950, may now be extinct in East Africa since a planting of sisal covers the area whence it came. It was collected at Magunga in the foothills of the Usambara Mountains, and appears to be closely related to grotei, also from those mountains.

The flowers, in clusters of 2 to 4, are Violet 4 (New England Gladiolus Chart) with a darker V 2 center. The rounded leaves with crenate margins, cupped under a little, are medium green above and pale greenish white below, with midribs prominent. The petioles are 3-7 cm. long and 3-6 cm. wide. The stems are "procumbent, branched, rooting where they come in contact with soil, pale greenish when young and developing a brownish, corky outer layer when older, 6-14 cm. long." The vegetative parts of the plant are covered with long and short hairs, inter mixed.

Mr. Roberts notes that S. magungensis differs from grotei "in having much smaller leaves, shorter petioles, crenate rather than dentate-crenate leaf margins, nonglandular hairs on margin of corolla, unlobed stigma, and darker flower color. All three of these procumbent species, like S. diplotricha B. L. Burtt, have a pubescence composed of hairs of two different lengths, intermixed.

"S. magungensis with its creeping, branching stems and its beautiful leaves cupping downward is indeed a valuable addition to the genus. It has an artistic habit of growing over the sides of the container . . . Possible future hybrids of it will undoubtedly have other colors . . . One of its hybrids has already developed into one of the most erect African Violet plants in existence in spite of the fact that S. magungensis is a creeping type . . . with branching stems. The possibilities are numerous."

SAINTPAULIA PUSILLA ENGLER

Also found by W. Goetz and described by Professor Engler in his *Botanische Jahrbücher* is this smallest of the species known to date. It is a true miniature, apparently measuring but 5 inches across, and so of inestimable value to breeders interested in developing window-sill types. Saintpaulia pusilla may still be found growing on large boulders among moss "in the primeval forests of the central Uluguru mountains, on the south side of the Lukwangule plateaus, 1200 to 1800 meters."

The tiny flowers are bicolor, light blue and white, and the

petals are "narrowly triangular." The capsule is elongated at the base. The small leaves are obtuse at both ends and violet-colored beneath.

SAINTPAULIA TONGWENSIS B. L. BURTT

This species was discovered at an altitude of 2300 feet on a fifty-yard ledge of rock on the ridge of Mt. Tongwe. The area was surrounded by a barrier of five-foot grass, which evidently kept tongwensis pure. It has not been distributed nor have seeds of other species penetrated the grass to effect crosses. H. B. Herring discovered the plant "growing in humus on gneiss rocks beneath a light shade of undergrowth. (B. L. Burtt described tongwensis in 1947.) In cultivation it flowers better at 80 to 90 degrees F. than at 65 to 75 degrees, although it blooms satisfactorily in the cooler range.

The flowers, 1⅛ inches across, in clusters of 4 or 5, are light blue, almost as pale as Tinted Lady and not so deep as Blue Eyes. Plants bloom freely with plenty of space between flower stems.

The leaf is rather transparent, heart-shaped, and dentate, measuring 2 by 3¼ inches. Multicellular hairs appear on older ones. There is a broad pale band along the center, running parallel to the midrib. This characteristic is particularly noticeable under artificial light. Petioles grow to 3½ inches and have spreading hairs. Seed pods are cylindrical, ½ to ¾ of an inch long.

The pale tint of tongwensis and the banded leaf are of interest to the breeder.

CHAPTER ELEVEN

Infinite Variety

No pleasure endures unseasoned by variety.
PUBLICUS SIGNIS, CIRCA 42 B.C.

A decade or so ago, the collecting of saintpaulias was a pleasant, restful undertaking. But one species, S. ionantha, was recognized, and if you had ten different varieties, you had something pretty special. Today there are literally hundreds of varieties, really too many in view of the present possibilities of keeping them straight, and there is no end in sight. Not that there should be, provided that each saintpaulia introduced is really a fixed variety, capable of being reproduced, and with a name all its own and not one used in some other part of the country for some other variety, perhaps already widely known.

In 1948, the African Violet Society published in their *Magazine* a number of exact descriptions, so that the well-known older varieties are now easy to recognize. I gave those complete descriptions in the Revision of my first book, and they are excellent. Since 1948, a multitude of other varieties have been registered through publication in the *Magazine*, and Mr. Neil C. Miller has supplied me with their descriptions from the registration

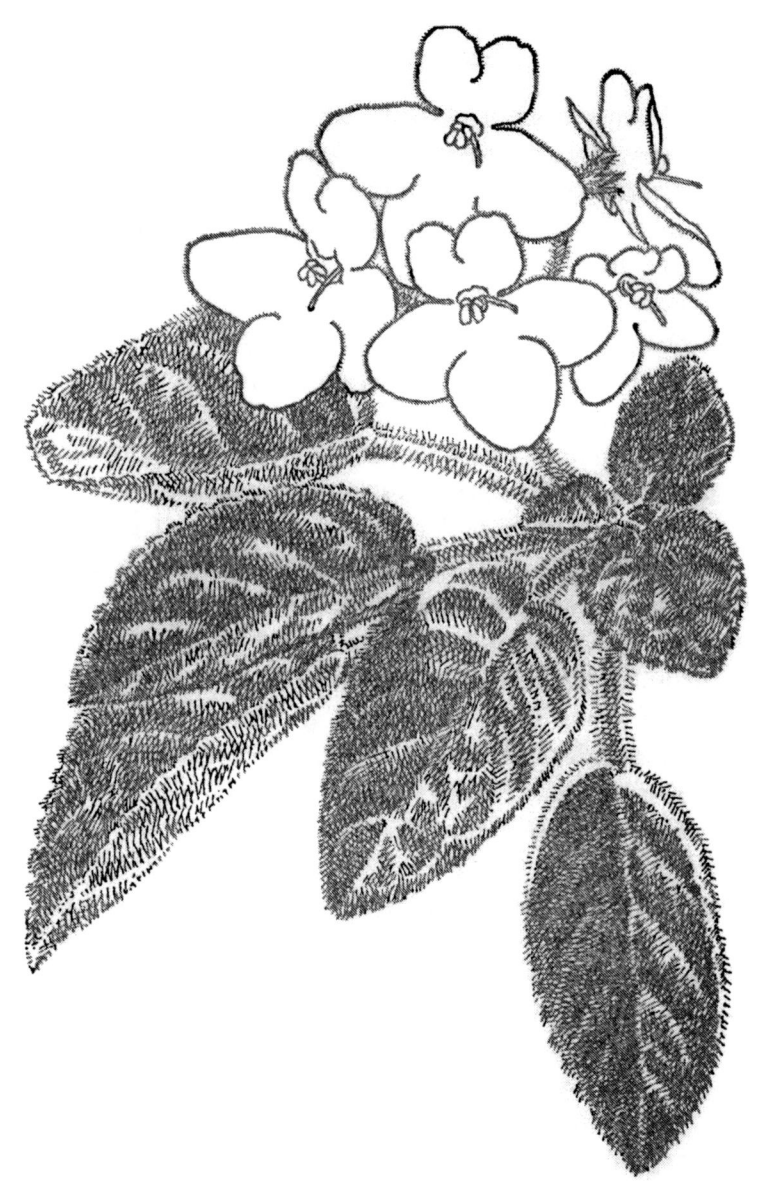

S. ionantha, a Spooned Type

cards. Many other names appear on my list, which is complete to the best of my present-day knowledge. Many of these varieties I have seen in growers' greenhouses, many in private collections. A number have been described for me by collectors whose opinions I value.

There is, of course, no such thing as a permanent list, not for this fast-moving lady, our African violet. We must always be willing to substitute new varieties for some of the poorer old ones, and improved strains, when these are available. In view of the intensive amateur and professional breeding programs, we can expect many fine new and unusual types to appear.

The fascinating doubles have been developed since the 1948 descriptions were given, the range of duPonts has been handsomely extended, and more recently the beautiful break, known as the Fringettes, has given collectors great pleasure. New patterns of foliage are here in Lacy Girl, Sea Queen and Bronze Queen, and Variegateds with marbled, striped, dotted, and rimmed flowers. Fantasy is an example of marbling. Lady Geneva is blue with a white edge. Twinkle Girl is a single white with a *vivid* blue edge, Lady Ulery a double white with a blue edge. Dark Beauty is a blue double with white shadings, and Star-of-Bethlehem a lovely dark blue with a white center.

There are already certain recognized strains. Any variety may, for instance, develop what are termed duPont, Supreme, Leatherneck, or Amazon characteristics. Almost any plant may be "spooned," or produce leaves of an exaggerated cupped form, as in the drawing of Spooned Neptune.

The Supremes are mutations of varieties whose names carry the extra descriptive term, as Blue Boy Supreme. Foliage is usu-

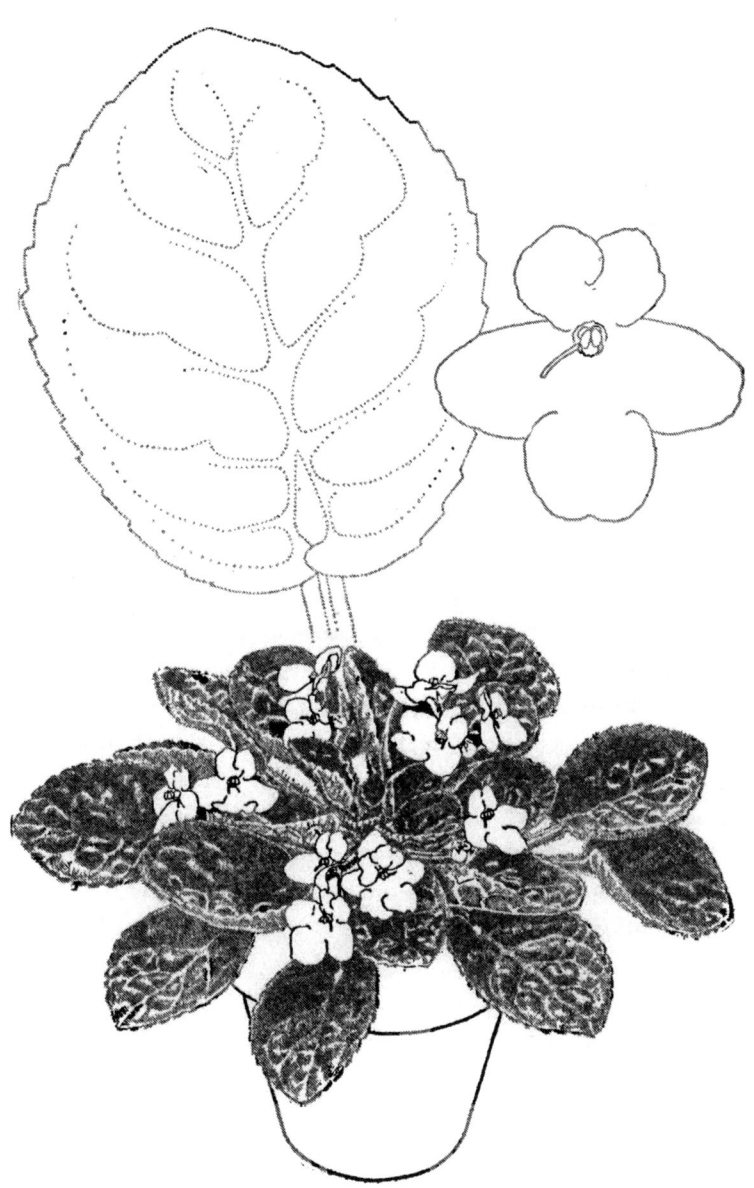

Neptune, with Spooned Foliage

ally brittle and heavier, while displaying the same varietal pattern. Flowers are not so freely borne, but they are larger than the variety normally produces. The duPont strain is characterized by thick, hairy, quilted leaves, somewhat curled and with a piecrust edge. It is slow-growing, not very prolific, but when in bloom produces very large flowers crowded on a few stems. Flowers may measure 2½ to 3 inches across. Good & Reese Inc. of Ohio, produced in 1949 a beautiful numbered series—the duPont Blue Hybrids. Mrs. William K. duPont will long be remembered for the contributions which originated in her greenhouses in Wilmington. She named only two, Christina and Blue Delaware. Both are lovely.

The Leatherneck strain, developed by R. A. Brown in Georgia, is characterized by smooth leaf edges and flexible growth, which, being pliable, travels better.

The Amazons, also from the Browns, are very like duPonts, but the Browns report that the leaves incline "to cup down slightly and in the blue series the leaf edges are dentate."

Certain characteristics seem possible for almost any variety. An all-white stalk or a few all-white leaves are not evidence of a true albino. Plants with very light sections often lack vitality and the departure does not survive as fixed. There is usually little stamina or longevity in the pale areas of growth.

Variegation of foliage may appear on any saintpaulia depending on cultural conditions, but the characteristic sometimes sticks as in Blue Girl, Pink Girl, and Orchid Girl. These varieties always have an irregular green-yellow to white area at the leaf base.

The tendency to doubleness may come and go. A plant will

Orchid Beauty, Hanging-Basket Type

SAINTPAULIA

CLASS V	White	
	Snow Prince, White Lady	

CLASS II	BV. 6 Pale Blue Violet	V. 6 Pale Lavender
	Sailor Boy, Tinted Lady	Blue-Eyed Beauty, Mauve Fringette
	BV. 5 Very Light Blue Violet	V. 5 Light Lavender
	Amazon Blue Eyes, S. ionantha, Sailor Girl	Amethyst, Jessie, Violet Beauty
	BV. 4 Light Blue Violet	V. 4 Lavender
	America, S. diplotricha, Marine Bouquet	Myrtle, Pale Orchid Double

CLASS I	BV. 3 Medium Blue Violet	V. 3 Medium Purple
	Crinkles, du Pont Blue, Norseman	Blue Boy, Neptune
	BV. 2 Blue Violet	V. 2 Purple
	Bluebird, Mammoth Blue, Helen Wilson	Commander, Double Margaret, Purple Girl
	BV. 1 Intense Blue Violet	V. 1 Intense Purple
	Lacy Girl, Navy Bouquet, Viking	Purple Prince

Five classifications in a comparative color sequence based on actual flower tint gradations of freshly picked blossoms. Numbers 1, 2, 3, indi-

Saintpaulia Color Chart

COLOR CHART

White
Snow Prince, White Lady

RV.6 Pale Lavender Pink	**R.6 Pale Pink**
Bicolor, du Pont Lavender Pink	*Blush Supreme, Blushing Maiden*
RV.5 Light Lavender Pink	**R.5 Light Pink**
Lavender Girl, Rainbow Geneva	*Tinari's Pink Luster*
RV.4 Lavender Pink	**R.4 Pink**
Mammoth Red, Redland	*Amazon Pink, Pink Beauty*
RV.3 Medium Red Violet	**R.3 Rose**
Burgundy, Plum Satin, Ruby Bouquet	
RV.2 Red Violet	**R.2 Carmine**
Frieda, Red King	
RV.1 Intense Red Violet	**R.1 Intense Carmine**
Wine Velvet	

CLASS III   CLASS IV

cate deeper colors; 4, 5, 6, indicate paler tints, fading to 7, or white. (Some color sections still lack available representative varieties.)

Saintpaulia Color Chart

bear some flowers with twice the petals of the rest. However, in Double Blue Boy, in the double purple Helen Wilson, in the lovely double white, Alma Wright, and in the Tinari's appealing Bouquet Series, doubleness stays.

There is the same variability in two-toned flowers. In many flowers the upper petals are noticeably lighter or darker than the lower ones but after blossoms are open a few days, the bicolor tendency may disappear. Furthermore, on some plants it will not show on every blossom. In Bicolor, however, the tendency is fixed and is transmitted to offspring. Varieties of two colors, rather than of two tones, are apparently in the making.

We find also that there are saintpaulias of miniature growth. When well-grown and mature, they are still of more limited size than the majority of African violets. Tear Drop, a medium blue from Fischer's is to me one of the most attractive of all violets. You will see a picture of it among the colored illustrations following page 128. Note its comparative smaller size. I always think of Tear Drop as "a winsome plant." Mrs. Ferne Kellar and Mrs. F. W. Gammell of Iowa have developed the "Violette" series of miniatures—Pixie, Bronze Baby, and Bronze Elf with interesting foliage patterns. Their Rosette Red has leaves suggestive of calla lilies.

There is also a general tendency to a hanging-basket type of plant, sometimes called pick-a-back, like the Orchid Beauty on page 189. Such plants rarely develop outside a greenhouse. Perhaps they display a characteristic latent in all saintpaulias. In the three species, S. grotei, amaniensis, and magungensis, the creeping tendency is more obvious.

COLOR

The color of saintpaulias is a not too constant quality. In fact, it seems to me after we decide saintpaulias have a range from deep, intense purples through blue-violets, wine-red, and pink-violets to pink, blush, and white, that we have about told the color story. To give each variety a symbol and place it exactly on a finely graded chart is hardly possible or worth while. I have tried this method with several charts and at different seasons. It was a frustrating business. The saintpaulia which today is Red Violet 4, may after a week of cloudy weather be nearer Red Violet 6. The variety which in one soil is blue under more alkaline conditions may be orchid. We must never be arbitrary about color.

Perhaps it is best to think of color as a relative characteristic—Viking will always be deeper than Blue Eyes, but the degree of variance may not be constant. In view of saintpaulia variability, I have discarded the symbols used in my first book and am describing colors only with words. My Color Chart is for tentative guidance only, although it was developed from an *actual sequence* of flowers picked from plants in full bloom and arranged on a table according to gradation of color.

In describing saintpaulias, we should use botanical terms, as cordate, ovate, etc. These present a true and vivid picture. In Saintpaulia Language and the drawing of Typical Leaf Forms on page 193, you will find simple explanations and pictures to illustrate this accepted plant terminology and also the special vocabulary we have adopted in our discussions of African violets.

OVATE
Amethyst
NARROW OVATE
Ruffles
BROAD OVATE
Blue Boy Supreme
OBOVATE
Sp. Neptune.
CORDATE
Orchid Beauty
ROUND
du Pont Lavender Pink
RHOMBIC
Pink Beauty
CRENATE
Almost entire; small; large shallow; large deep
Commando; S. ionantha: Plum; Blue Girl
SCALLOPED
Small shallow; large deep
Pink Beauty; du Pont Blue
BENT
White Lady
WAVY
Ruffles
SPOONED
Spooned Neptune
TROUGHED
Amethyst

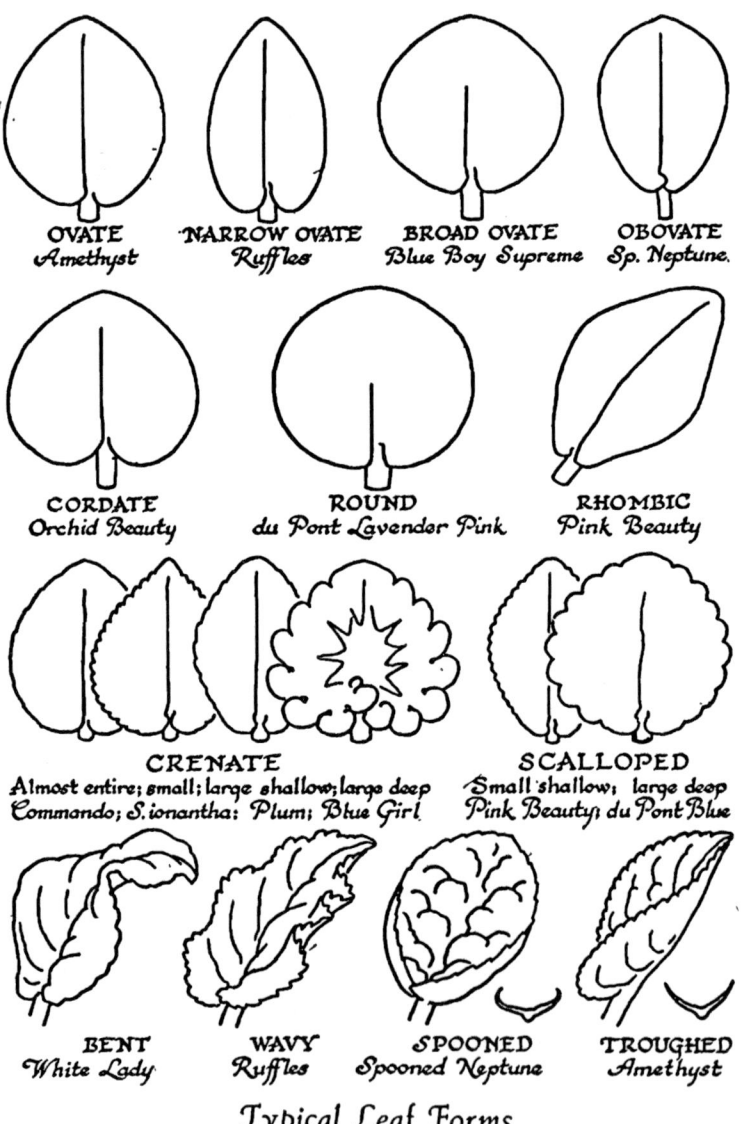

Typical Leaf Forms

A "Complete" List of Varieties with Synonyms

Here are the names of every African violet ever christened—at least to my knowledge. Here are the oldest varieties classified, the newest ones catalogued, and all varieties registered to date. At first it was my purpose to describe every one, but after writing some 400 descriptions, I decided it was unwise at this stage of classification since the varieties cherished today may be outmoded tomorrow. When a little of the present naming furor has died down, when the public itself has done its usual competent job of discarding and approving, then I will attempt descriptions. So here is a complete listing with all the synonyms I knew or could discover. As duplicates come to your attention, I hope you will write me (in care of my publisher in New York), so that I can constantly revise this list and make it ever more useful for growers and collectors.

Where duplicate names exist, there is a cross reference. *See* is used after the favorite or accepted name. *Also known as* indicates that other names follow, but none is so acceptable. *The same as* refers to names of equal acceptance, as Jessie and West Coast Amethyst. (See Index for page numbers of illustrations.)

Admiral (Also known as Irene)
Admiration
Afterglow
Agate (See Neptune)
Albino
Alice Blue Gown
Alma's Blue (See Sailor Boy)
Alma Wright
Amarantha
Amazon Blue Eyes (Illustrated in color)
Amazon Blue Girl
Amazon Giant Blue
Amazon Neptune
Amazon Old Lace
Amazon Pink (See Pink Supreme)
Amazon Pink Lace
Amazon Purple Prince (Illustrated in color on cover)
Amazon Red
Amethyst (Also known as Dark Amethyst, Lavender Lady, Light Orchid, Orchid Lady; illustrated)
Amethyst Amazon
Amethyst Beauty
Amethyst Pink (See Jessie)
Anemone Double

Apollo (Illustrated in color)
Apple Blossom
Azure Beauty
Azure Glory
Baby Blue
Baby Blue Eyes (See Sailor Boy)
Baby Girl Spoon
Beauty Girl
Begonia Bell (See Blue Bird)
Begonia Blue (See Blue Bird)
Behnke Boy
Betty Joe (See Orchid Beauty)
Beverly
Bicolor (Also known as Red Bicolor; illustrated in color on frontispiece and in drawing)
Bicolor duPont
Big Boy
Big Mike
Bit O' Heaven
Black Beauty (Also known as Mentor Boy Supreme)
Black Ruby
Blue Amazon (See Blue Boy Supreme)
Blue and White
Blue Angel

Amethyst

Blue Barbara
Blue Beany
Blue Beauty
Bluebelle
Blue Bird (Also known as Begonia Blue, Begonia Bell, Twilight; illustrated)
Blue Bobby
Blue Bonnet (See Blue Girl)
Blue Boy (Illustrated in color on frontispiece and in drawing)
Blue Boy Improved
Blue Boy Profuse (See Blue Boy)
Blue Boy Supreme (Also known as Blue Amazon; illustrated)
Blue Butterfly
Blue Chard (Illustrated in color on frontispiece and in drawing)
Blue Dainty Maid
Blue Darling (See Blue Boy)
Blue Delaware
Blue Delphinium
Blue Diamond
Blue Dream
Blue duPont #4
Blue-Eyed Beauty
Blue-Eyed Girl
Blue Eyes (See Tinari's Blue Eyes)
Blue Fantasy
Blue Frills
Blue Girl (Also known as Blue Bonnet; illustrated in color on frontispiece and in drawing. Patented)
Blue Girl Compacta
Blue Girl Hybrid
Blue Girl Supreme
Blue Heaven
Blue Hydrangea
Blue Jane
Blue King
Blue Knight
Blue Lady
Blue Lavender Fringette
Blue Leatherneck
Blue Longifolia Crenulate
Blue Mammoth
Blue Marion
Blue Missy
Blue Moiré
Blue Monday
Blue Moon
Blue No. 32

Bicolor

Blue Bird

Blue Boy

Blue No. 3 (See Blue Treasure)
Blue Perfection
Blue Pet
Blue Rosette
Blue Scoop (also known as Chicago Scoop)
Blue Skies (See Tinari's Blue Eyes)
Blue Snow
Blue S-32
Blue Supreme
Blue Treasure (Also known as Blue No. 3)
Blue Velvet
Blue Violet (See S. ionantha)
Blue Waterlily
Blush (See Blushing Maiden)
Blush Beauty (See Blushing Maiden)
Blush Supreme (also known as Blush)
Blushing Lady (See Blushing Maiden)
Blushing Maiden (Also known as Blush, Blush Beauty, Blushing Lady, and Maiden's Blush)
Blushing Maiden Supreme (Illustrated in color on frontispiece)
Blynken
Bonita
Bonny Girl
Bouquet Series (See specific names)
Bronze
Bronze Girl
Bronze Queen
Bronze Red Girl
Brown's Lilac Princess
Brown's Palmer Violet
Brown's Pet #2
Burgundy (Also known as My Lady Sue)
California Dark Plum
California Periwinkle
California Plum
Carter's Red (See Orchid Beauty)
Celestial Blue
Chalice
Charles
Charro
Chattanooga (See Mentor Boy)
Chicago Scoop (See Blue Scoop)
Christina

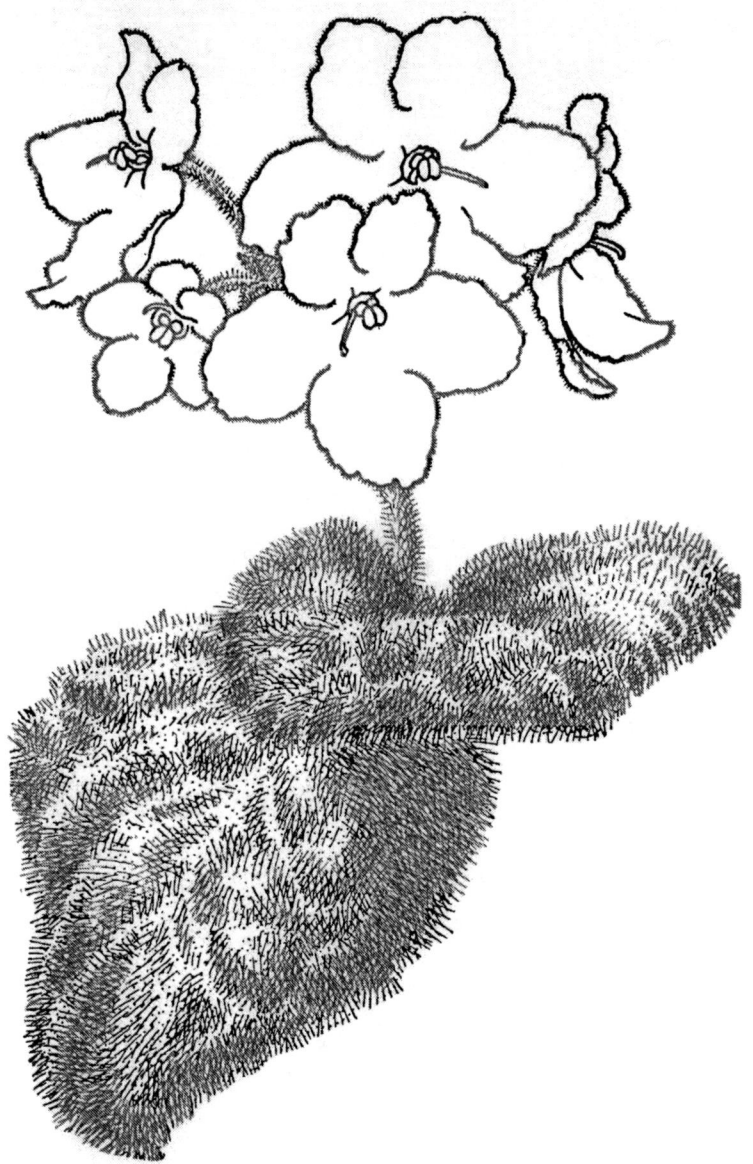

Blue Boy Supreme

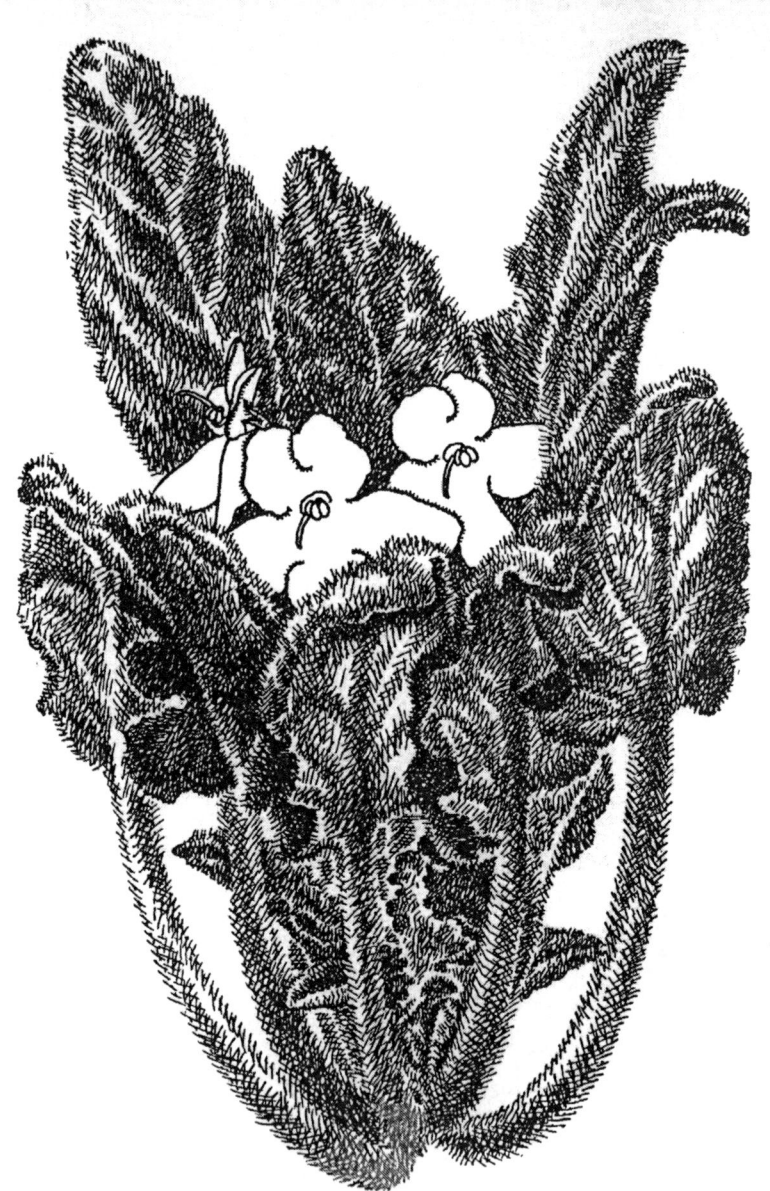

Blue Chard

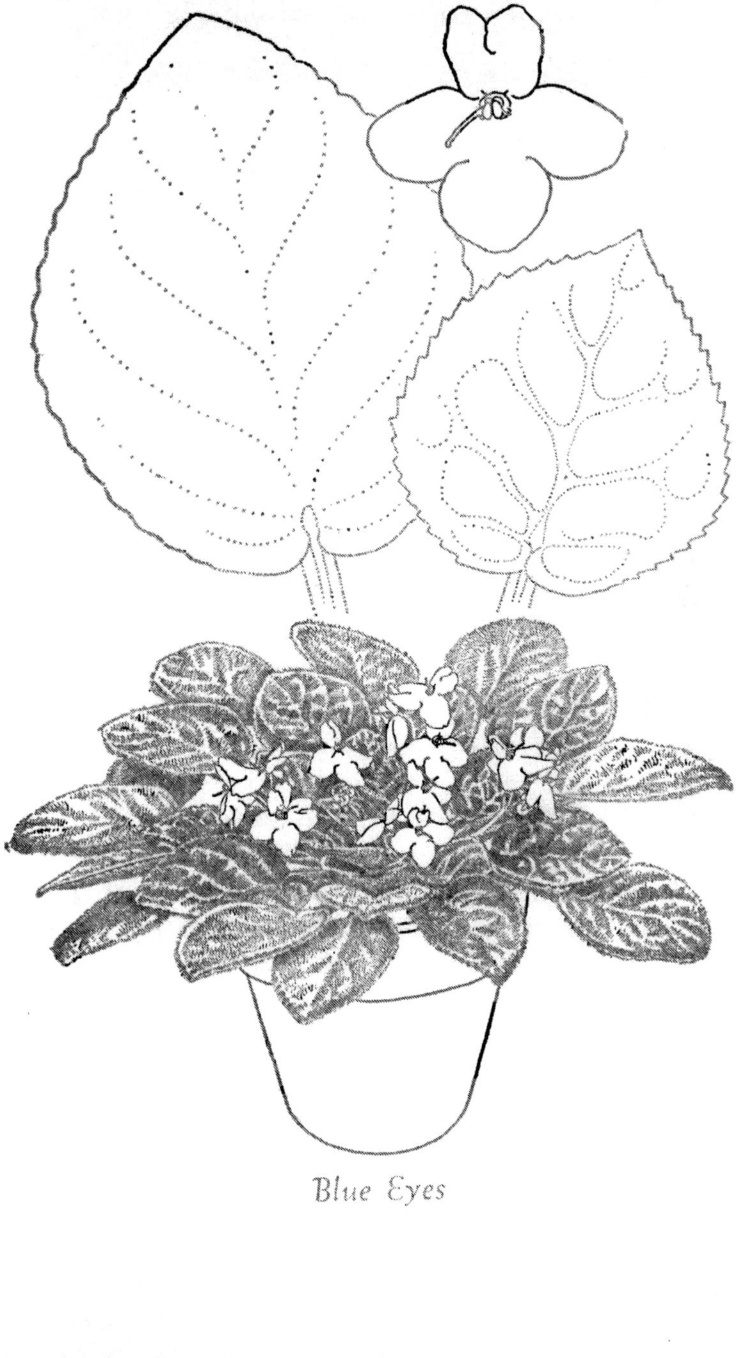

Blue Eyes

Commander (See Commodore)
Commando (See Commodore)
Commodore (Also known as Commander, Commando, Dickson's Purple, Imperial)
Congo Queen (See Red duPont)
Crazy Plum
Creation
Crinkles
Crystal Blue Double
Crystal Queen
Cupid
Curly Special (See Old Lace)
Curly Twist
Custard Cup
Dainty Lady
Dainty Maid (Also known as Pink Lady)
Dark Amethyst (See Amethyst)
Dark Blue Double Fringette
Dark Blue Fringette
Dark Blue Rosette
Dark Eyes
Dark Lavender
Dark Plum (See Plum Satin)
Dark Princess
Dark Red Head
Darling
Double Dark Lavender (See Double Orchid)
Double Light Blue
Double Light Lavender
Debutante
Delaware
Detroit (See White Girl)
Diana
Diane
Dickson's Purple (See Commodore)
S. diplotricha (Formerly S. kewensis)
Dixie Rose
Dorlene
Double Blue Boy (Also known as Double Dipper, Double Duchess, Double Purple, Double Russian, Double Wonder, Duchess, Silver Wings; illustrated)
Double Blue Boy Supreme
Double Doris
Double Dipper (See Double Blue Boy)
Double Duchess (See Double Blue Boy)

Blue Girl

Double Light Blue (See Fischer's Double Light Blue)
Double Margaret
Double Mary Wac (See Double Orchid)
Double Mentor Boy
Double Neptune (Also known as Queen Neptune)
Double Orchid (Also known as Double Mary Wac, Fischer's Masterpiece, Fischer's Double Dark Lavender, and Regal Wine)
Double Orchid Beauty
Double Orchid Lavender
Double Pink Beauty
Double Purple (See Double Blue Boy)
Double Russian (See Double Blue Boy)
Double Supreme
Double White
Double Wonder (See Double Blue Boy)
Dream Boat
Droopy (See Lancaster Red)
Dubonnet
Duchess (See Double Blue Boy)
DuPont Blue (Illustrated)
DuPont Blue Hybrids No. 1 to No. 5
DuPont Lavender Pink (Also known as duPont Pink; illustrated in color and in drawing)
DuPont Pink (See duPont Lavender Pink)
DuPont Red
DuPont Silver Pink
DuPont Tu-Tone (See Red Supreme)
DuPont, W. K.
Dwarf Orchid Beauty
Dwarf Topaz
Elite
Emily Jane
Emperor Wilhelm
Enchantress
Fischer's Masterpiece (See Double Orchid)
Flamingo Girl
Florida Lady
Fontana
Forget-me-not
Evening Star
Fairy Princess

Double Blue Boy

Fantasy (also known as Freckles; illustrated in color)
Fern Leaf Blue
Freckles (See Fantasy)
Frieda (also known as Red Ionantha)
Fringette Series
Fuchsia Spoon
Garnet (See Orchid Beauty)
Gatton Blue
Gatton Purple
Gay Lark
Geneva Rainbow
Georgia Belle
Giant Light Blue
Giant Red Lavender
Giant Rose Pink
Glorious
Good's Orchid (See Orchid Beauty)
Gorgeous (also known as Grand Lady)
Gorgeous Bicolor
Gorgeous Gal
Gorgeous Spoon Leaf (Patented)
Gorgeous Spoon Leaf Variegated
Grand Lady (See Gorgeous)
Gray Lady (See Tinted Lady)
Guam
Gwen
Gypsy Ann
Gypsy Appleblossom
Gypsy Crown
Gypsy Freak
Gypsy Jane
Gypsy Jewel
Gypsy King
Gypsy Lace
Gypsy Prince
Gypsy Queen
Gypsy Rose
Gypsy Rosa
Gypsy Rubra
Halo
Hardee Blue
Harmon
Heart's Desire
Heavenly Blue
Helen Wilson (see Tinari's Helen Wilson)
Helen Wilson Bouquet
Holbrook Blue
Holbrook Red (See Plum Satin)
Hoosier Beauty
Hoosier Maid

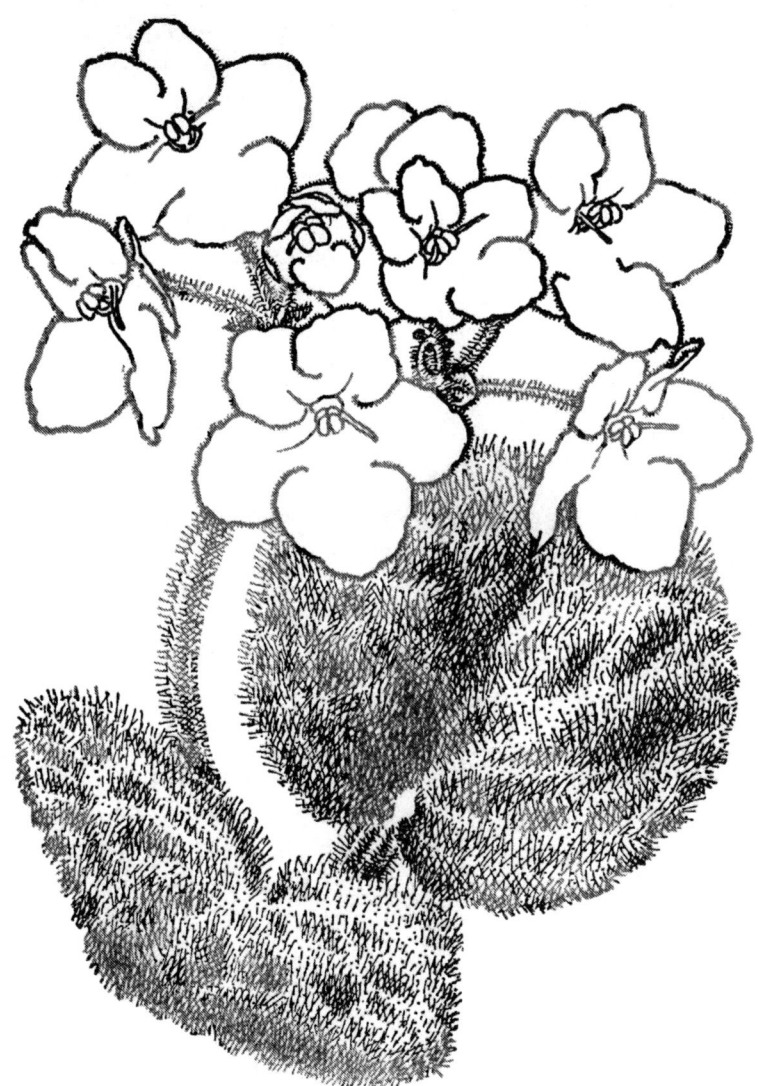

DuPont Blue

Hoosier Sport
Hope
Hyacinth Blue
Ida Blue
Imperial (See Commodore)
Indian Chief
Irene (See Admiral)
Iridescent
Ison
Jack Frost
Jade
Janie's Blue
J. A. Thomas
Jessie (Also known as West Coast Amethyst, Pink Amethyst, Zig)
Jinaro
Joel's Delight
Jo-Li-An
Judy
Junette
Kay's Quilted
S. kewensis (see S. diplotricha)
Lacy Bouquet
Lacy Girl
Lady Bette
Lady Catherine
Lady Constance
Lady Geneva (Illustrated in color. Patented)
Lady Marion (See Neptune)
Lady Slipper
Lancaster Red (Also known as Droopy, Red Spoon)
Larkspur
Lavender Double
Lavender Afterglow
Lavender Beauty
Lavender Bicolor
Lavender Frills
Lavender Girl
Lavender Lady (See Amethyst)
Lavender Lady Supreme
Lavender Neptune
Lavender Pink
Lavender Pink Princess
Leslie
Light Blue Double Fringette
Light Blue
Light Blue Fringette
Light Blue Girl (See Sailor Girl)
Light Blue Moiré
Light Lavender Rosette
Light Orchid (See Amethyst)
Lilac Beauty

DuPont Lavender Pink

Lilac Lady
Lilac Lass
Lilac Princess
Lily Pad
Lithium (See Summer Skies)
L. M. Byrnes Blue
Lois
Lorene (See Neptune)
Love Birds
Luana
Lucky Girl
McFarland's Blue Warrior
Maiden's Blush (See Blushing Maiden)
Mammoth Blue
Mammoth Red
Mardi-Fuchsia
Mardi's Bicolor
Mardi's Purple
Marie Antoinette
Marine
Marine Bouquet
Marine Supreme
Marionette
Marmaduke
Marmarata
Maroon
Maroon Brocade
Martha Lou

Mary
Mary's Orchid
Mary Sue
Mary Wac (See Orchid Beauty)
Mauve (See Plum Satin)
Mauve Fringette (Also known as Pale Mauve Lavender Fringette; illustrated in color)
Mauve Lace
Mauvette Lavender Fringette
May Day
May Greer
Mentor Boy (Also known as Chattanooga, Purple Mist, Pansy Purple)
Mentor Boy Amazon
Mentor Boy Supreme (See Black Beauty)
Merkel's Blue Brilliant
Merkel's Giant Blue
Merkel's Light Blue
Merkel's Medium Blue
Merkel's No. II
Merkel's Red
Merkel's Red Purple (See Purple Prince)
Merkel's Red Ripples

Norseman

Merkel's Wax Blue
Mermaid
Midnight
Mi-Jo
Mildred's Choice
Miss Harriet
Miss Liberty
Misty Blue
Moiré
Moonbeam
Moonglow
Morning Star
Mottled White
Mrs. Boles
Mrs. Emery
Mrs. Evelyn Banks
Mrs. Stratton
Mulberry Girl
Multiflora
My Lady Carol
My Lady Elizabeth
My Lady Frances
My Lady Joan
My Lady Marion
My Lady Sharon
My Lady Sue (Also known as Burgundy)
My Love
Myrtle

My Second Prize
Naughty Marietta
Navy Bouquet
Neptune (Also known as Agate, Lady Marion, and Lorene; illustrated in color, also spooned type in drawing)
Neptune Princess
Neptune Supreme
New Blue
New Double Purple
Nod
Norseman (Illustrated)
Norseman Bouquet
Norseman Supreme
Nosegay
No. 32
Nyla Jean
Old Lace (Also known as Curly Special)
Old Rose
Orchid Ballerina
Orchid Ballet
Orchid Beauty (Also known as Betty Joe, Carter's Red, Garnet, Good's Orchid, Mary Wac, Orchid Queen, Orchid Red, Plum, Plum

Orchid Beauty

Pink, Plum Vivid, Rosy Blue, Trilby, and Vivid; illustrated)
Orchid Beauty Amazon
Orchid Beauty, Dwarf (See Dwarf Orchid Beauty)
Orchid Beauty Supreme
Orchid Big-Boy
Orchid Bicolor
Orchid Compacta
Orchid Eyes
Orchid Flute
Orchid Girl (also known as Red Head Girl)
Orchid Lady (See Amethyst)
Orchid Neptune
Orchid Prince
Orchid Queen (See Orchid Beauty)
Orchid Red (See Orchid Beauty)
Orchid Supreme
Orchid Wonder
Oriental
Oriental Girl
Ozark Skies (See Norseman)
Pacific Prince
Painted Ballerina

Pale Mauve Lavender Fringette (See Mauve Fringette)
Pale Mauve Fringette
Pale Orchid Double
Pansy
Pansy Purple (See Mentor Boy)
Pansy Purple Supreme
Pastel Girl
Patricia
Periwinkle
Peter Pan
Petite
Pied Piper
Pink Amethyst (see Jessie)
Pink Beauty (Also known as Pink Perfection, Pink Princess, and Pinky; illustrated in color and in drawing. Patented)
Pink Beauty Supreme (Patented)
Pink Cutie
Pink Girl
Pink Lace
Pink Lady (see Dainty Maid)
Pink Leatherneck
Pink Perfection (See Pink Beauty)

Orchid Beauty (Detail)

Pink Princess (See Pink Beauty)
Pink Star (See Star Pink)
Pink Supreme (Apparently same as Amazon Pink)
Pinky (See Pink Beauty)
Plum (See Orchid Beauty)
Plum Pink (See Orchid Beauty)
Plum Satin (also known as Mauve, Holbrook Red, Dark Plum)
'lum Vivid (See Orchid Beauty)
Polka Dot
Princess Leila
Purity
Purple Beauty
Purple Bouquet
Purple Gem
Purple Girl
Purple Mist (See Mentor Boy)
Purple Prince (Also known as Merkel's Red Purple)
Purple Shadows
Queen Neptune (See Double Neptune)
Queen of Hearts
Radiant

Radiant Shantilly
Raggedy Ann
Rainbow Geneva
Ranee
Red Amazon (See Red Supreme)
Red Amethyst
Red Beauty
Red Bicolor (See Bicolor)
Red Bird
Red Dainty Maid
Red Dawn
Red Duke
Red duPont (Also known as Congo Queen)
Red Feather
Red Frills
Red Girl
Red Girl Hybrid
Red Head (Illustrated in color on frontispiece)
Red Head Girl (See Orchid Girl)
Red Head Supreme
Red Ionantha (See Frieda)
Red King (Illustrated in color)
Redland
Red Lavender Fringette
Red Moiré

Pink Beauty

Red Pet
Red Prince
Red Queen
Red Ruffles
Red Spoon (See Lancaster Red)
Red Supreme (Also known as Red Amazon, duPont Tu-Tone)
Red Surprise
Red Waves
Regal Rose
Regal Wine (See Double Orchid)
Rhodes No. 1 (See S. ionantha)
Rippling Blue
Rosalie
Rosebud
Rose Chimes
Rose Marie
Rose Onna Maple
Rose Onna Swirl
Rose Pink
Rose Purple
"Rosette" Red
Rosita
Rosy Blue (See Orchid Beauty)
Rosy O'Grady
Rosy Red
Royal
Royal Rose
Royal Sunset (See Viking)
Ruby Bouquet
Ruffled White
Ruffles (Illustrated)
Saffron Red Boy
Sailor Boy (Also known as Alma's Blue, Baby Blue Eyes)
S. amaniensis, Species
S. diplotricha, Species
S. diplotricha Supreme
S. goetzeana, Species
S. grotei, Species
S. ionantha, Species (Also known as ionantha grandiflora, ionantha Improved, Blue Violet, Rhodes No. 1; illustrated.)
S. ionantha Improved (See S. ionantha)
S. ionantha grandiflora (See S. ionantha)
S. ionantha Supreme
S. kewensis Supreme (See S. diplotricha Supreme)

Ruffles

S. magungensis
S. pusilla
S. tongwensis
Sailor Girl
Sailor Girl #1
Salem Maiden
Sally Mac
Sapphire (Illustrated)
"Seafoam" Sea Queen
Sea Girl
Semi-Double
Semi-Double Blue Bouquet
Semi-Dwarf Fringette
Chantilly
Sharon
Sherri
Show Girl
Shrimpie
Silver Wings (See Double Blue Boy)
Sky Blue (See Tinted Lady)
Sky Blue Supreme
Snow Girl
Snow Prince (Illustrated in color on cover)
Snow Princess
Snow Queen
Snow Storm
Soldier Boy

Spoon Girl
Starlight (also known as Swinburne's Delight, Waterlily; illustrated)
Star-of-Bethlehem
Star Pink
Star Sapphire
S-32 Bicolor
Storm King
Summer Skies (Also known as Lithium)
Sunrise
Sunset Lane
Supreme (See Viking)
Swinburne's Delight (See Starlight)
Swirling Girl
Tear Drop (Illustrated in color)
Thunderhead
Tex-Ann
Thirty-Two (Also known as No. 32)
Tinari's Amazon Blue Eyes
Tinari's America (Illustrated in color)
Tinari's Blue Eyes (Also known as Blue Eyes and Blue Skies; illustrated)

S. ionantha (Detail)

Sapphire

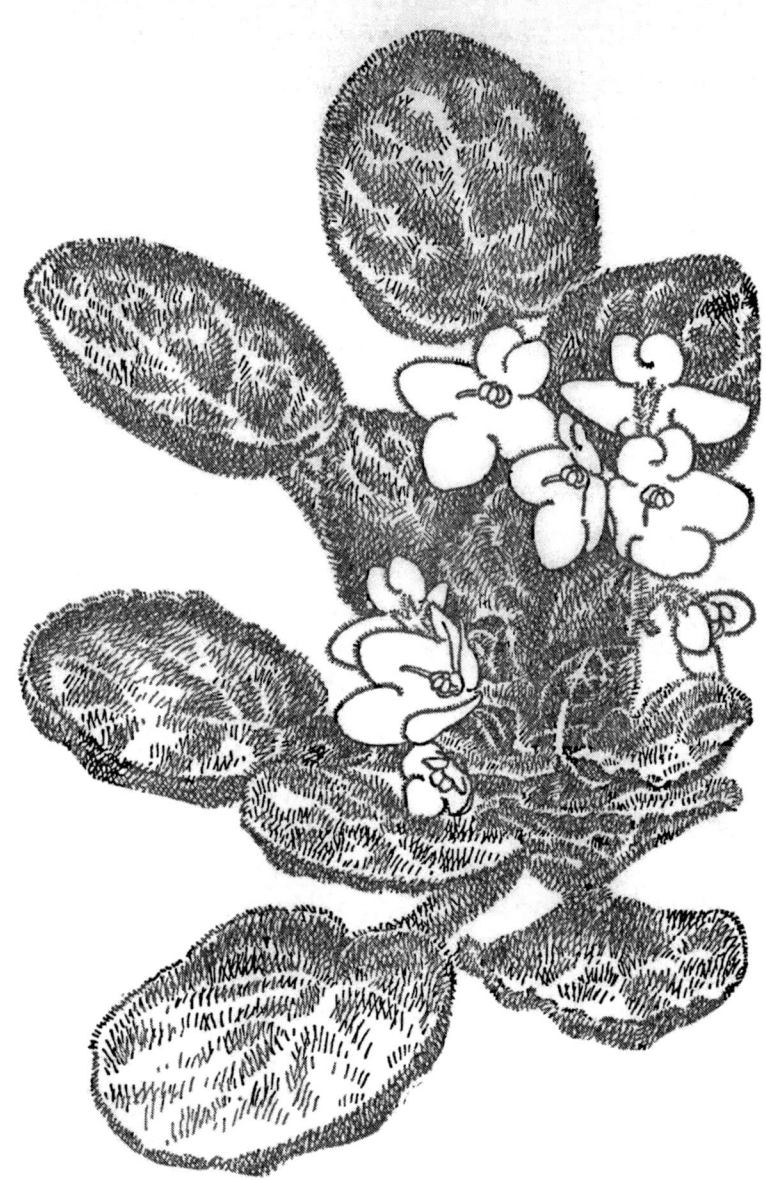

Starlight

Tinari's Blue Flute
Tinari's Double Mentor Boy
Tinari's Helen Wilson (Illustrated in color)
Tinari's Mammoth Blue
Tinari's Pink Luster (Illustrated in color on cover)
Tinari's Purple Prince Supreme
Tinted Lady (Also known as Gray Lady, Sky Blue)
Topaz (Also Topaz Sapphire)
Topaz Amazon
Trilby (See Orchid Beauty)
Tunia's Big Boy
Tunia's Cleveland Indian
Tunia's Prize Blue
Tunia's Red Butterfly
Tunia's Rose Butterfly
Turquoise
Tu-Tone Double
Tu-Tone Light Lavender
Twilight (See Blue Bird)
Twinkle Girl
Unique
Upjohn
Variegated Leaf Sport
Velvet Beauty
Velvet Bouquet
Vera Margaret
Viking (Also known as Royal Sunset and Supreme)
Violet Beauty (Illustrated in color)
Violette Baby Doll
Violette Bronze Baby
Violette Bronze Elf
Violette Pixie
Vivid (See Orchid Beauty)
Von Dietrich
Waterlily (See Starlight)
West Coast Amethyst (In the East known as Jessie)
Western Girl
White Amazon
White Beauty
White Boy
White Cap
White Enchantress
White Fringette (Illustrated in color)
White Girl (Also known as Detroit)
White Hybrid
White King
White Lady (Illustrated in color and in drawing. Patented)

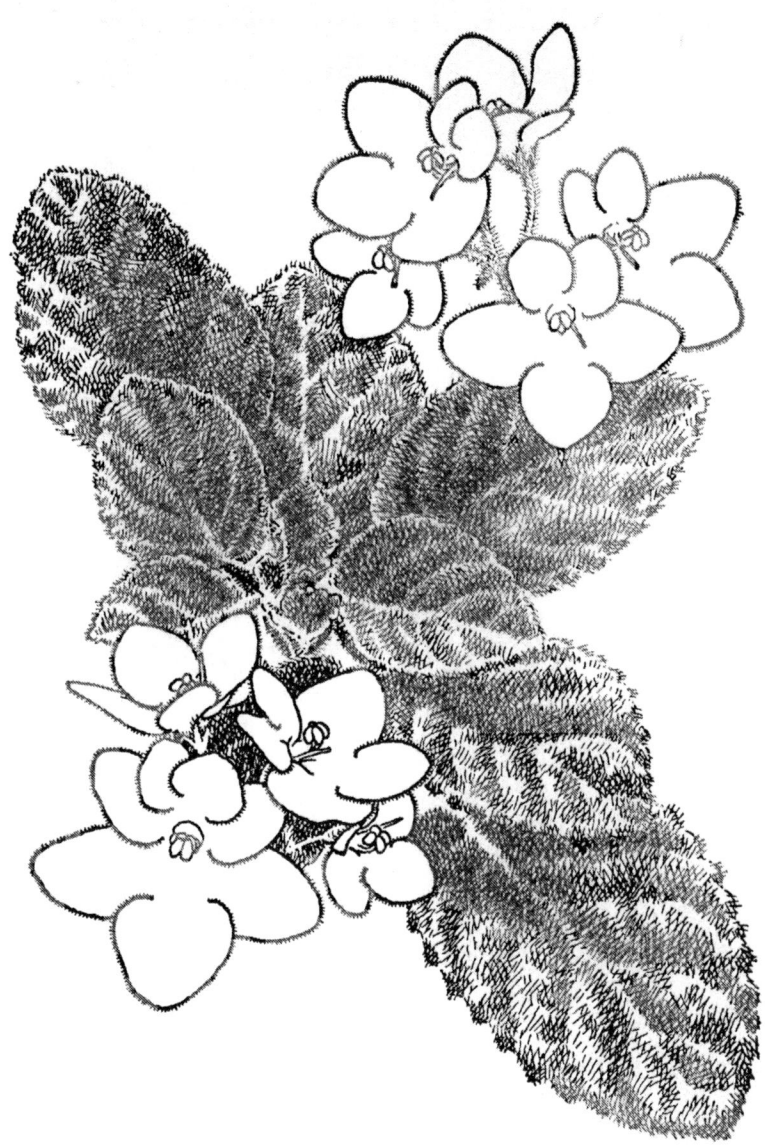

Viking

White Lady Supreme
White Lassie
White Orchid
White Pixie
White Prince
White Prize
White Queen
White Sister
White Supreme

White Waterlily (See Starlight)
White Wonder
Wine Velvet
Winifred Merkel
Wonder Star
Wynken
Zig (See Jessie)

White Lady

VARIETIES OF THE FUTURE

Saintpaulia Language

Acute. A leaf terminating in a sharp point.

Anther. The small sac carried on a thread emerging from the center of each flower. The anther splits to release pollen grains containing the male elements of the plant.

Calyx. The outer series of floral leaves. This external part is usually green in contrast to the inner showy portion, or corolla, composed of colored petals.

Capillary attraction. The apparent attraction between a solid and a liquid. Thus dry pots or dry soils moisten themselves by drawing on available sources of moisture. The glass-wick method of watering and watering from the saucer are based on this principle.

Chromosomes. Tiny hereditary bodies within the germ cells.

Clon or *Clone.* A plant and all its vegetative parts, as a saintpaulia variety and all the plants grown from cuttings of it.

Compost. Organic material, readily available to plants, because it has been thoroughly decomposed through fermentation brought about by the action of bacteria.

Cordate. A leaf form roughly heart-shaped and notched at the base.

Crenate. A leaf margin marked by rounded scallops.

Crock. A fragment of a broken, earthen flowerpot. If you fit a few overlapping pieces together in the bottom of a container to form a drainage area through which water but not soil will pass, you call it "crocking."

Cross-Pollination. The transfer of the pollen from the anthers of one variety to the stigma of another variety.

Cutting. A piece cut or broken from a parent plant for the purpose of obtaining additional plants of the identical type of the parent.

Dentate. A leaf with a toothed margin.

Entire. A smooth-edged leaf without grooves, scallops, or indentations of any kind.

Flat. A shallow box in which seeds or cuttings are started. The usual size is 16 by 22 inches with a 2- to 4-inch depth. Bottom boards are separated one-quarter inch to permit drainage.

Gene. A unit of inheritance involving but one single character.

Genus (Plural, genera). One subdivision of a plant family.

Germination. The first development of seeds into little plants. The rate of "bursting into life" depends not only on cultural factors but also on the innate disposition of the variety of the seeds.

Hybrid. (L. H. Bailey) "Any product of a cross when the parents were noticeably different from each other, whether the parents belonged to different clons, races, or species."

Hydroponics. The science of growing plants in a solution of chemicals and without soil.

Inorganic Fertilizer. A chemical product, artificially manufactured—nitrate of soda, ammonium sulphate, and muriate of potash.

Medium. The soil, sand, peatmoss, vermiculite, or mixture of any of these, in which seeds are sown or leaves rooted.

Midrib. The central vein of a leaf which appears as a ridge-like extension of the petiole or leaf stem.

Mutant. (Variant or Sport) An organism that has transmissible genic differences from the parent, and these differences (in the chromosome structure) are not due to crossing, but are changes brought about by nature.

Obovate. A leaf broader beyond the middle than at the base.

Obtuse. A leaf which is blunt rather than sharply pointed.

Organic Fertilizer. A fertilizer composed of once-living matter, as animal manure, blood, bone meal, hoof and horn meal; or vegetable residues—grass, leaves, stems, hay, cottonseed meal; or *natural* mineral products, as ground limestone, phosphate rock, etc.

Ovate. Egg-shaped leaves attached to their stems at the broad end. (Cf. cordate leaves which are similar but notched at the base where the petiole joins.)

Overpot. The use of a container large in relation to the earth ball it holds.

Pedicel. The section of the peduncle (flower stem) which supports the seed pod.

Peduncle. The stalk which supports a solitary flower or a cluster.

Petiole. The stalk by which a leaf is attached to a main stem.

Pinching. The act of nipping out with thumb and finger the end growth of a branch, or removing tight little buds to make remaining development fuller or to delay flowering.

Pistil. The ovule-bearing organ which receives pollen and, after fertilizing, develops seeds.

Plunge. The sinking of potted plants up to the pot rims in soil.

Pollen. The fertile, usually yellow, dust released from anthers.

Potbound. The condition of a plant whose roots are considerably restricted by the container in which it is growing. If the pot is lifted from such a plant, a mass of roots is revealed, covering the outside of the soil.

Rhombic-ovate. An oval leaf form widened through the center.

Sepal. A division of the calyx, that usually green cup which surrounds the colored petals.

Serrated. Notched or toothed on the edge like a saw.

Shifting. The moving of a plant to the next, larger-sized container with a little more soil but the least possible disturbance. This is in contrast to repotting which may involve replacement of worn-out soil with a fresh mixture, the improvement of drainage conditions, and even some cutting back of roots. Shifting is for healthy young plants on their way to maturity. Repotting is for established plants in need of reconditioning. In repotting, a larger pot may be provided, the same one used again, or even a smaller one selected, if the previous pot was overlarge.

Sinus. A point at the base of a leaf scallop or crenation.

Species. This is something nature produces, a group of plants sharing certain distinctive characteristics which indicate a common parent or genus. In plant designation, the first word indicates the genus, the second the species to which it belongs, and the third the variety, as Saintpaulia ionantha, Blue Boy.

Sport. (See Mutant.)

Stamen. The anther and the filament containing the male fertilizing cells.

Stigma. The part of the pistil of a flower which receives and holds the pollen grains and on which they germinate.

Sub-irrigation. Watering from the saucer or below the surface of the soil.

Systemic. An insecticide absorbed into the sap stream of a plant and "translocated" through the plant system, making it lethal to insects feeding on any part of a treated plant.

Variant. (See Mutant.)

Variety. The slight variation within a species which is noticeable but not important enough to constitute another species.

Index

See also varieties listed alphabetically, page 196ff.; terms defined in Saintpaulia Language, page 234ff.

A

Acidity, 33-34
Acute, definition of, 234
African Violet Magazine, The, 75, 139, 140, 173, 181, 184
African Violet Society of America, Inc., 20, 136-143, 154-155, 175, 178, 184
    classification by color, 146-149
    point scale, 146-147
    registration of variety, 75-76
Amaniensis E. P. Roberts, species, 176, 192, 222
    description of, 176
Amateur grower, definition of, 156
Amazon, 19, 157, 185, 188
Amazon Blue Eyes
    in color following page 128
Amazon Purple Prince, in color, cover
Amethyst, 138, 148, 156, 196
    illustration, 197
Anther, definition of, 234
Aphids or plant lice, 97, 99, 127
Apollo
    in color following page 128

B

Bailey, L. H., 64, 235
Bailey and Gilbert, *Plant Breeding*, 67

Baking-pan method of soil sterilization, 125
Benary, Ernst, 172-173, 176
Benary, Friedrich, 172
Bicolor, 46, 138, 148, 156, 192, 196, 220
    illustration, 199
    in color, frontispiece
Black flies, 123, 131
Black Leaf 40, 127
Bloom
    to produce, 17-46
    quantity of, 157
    size of, 157
Blue Amazon, see Blue Boy Supreme
Blue Bird, 138, 196, 198, 200
    illustration, 200
Blue Boy, 19, 34, 51, 53, 55, 70, 138, 147, 157, 198, 201
    illustration, 201
    in color, frontispiece
Blue Boy Improved, 138, 198
Blue Boy Supreme, 63, 147, 185, 186, 198
    illustration, 203
Blue Butterfly, 19, 198
Blue Chard, 198
    illustration, 204
    in color, frontispiece
Blue Delaware, 188, 198

INDEX

Blue-Eyed Beauty, 161, 198
Blue Eyes, see Tinari's Blue Eyes
Blue Girl, 34, 58, 59, 65, 138, 147, 159-161, 188, 198
  illustration, 207
  in color, frontispiece
Blue No. 32, 46, 198
Blue Velvet, 148, 202
Blue and White, 137, 196
Blush Beauty, see Blushing Maiden
Blushing Lady, see Blushing Maiden
Blushing Maiden (Blush Beauty, Blushing Lady), 138, 149, 161, 174, 196, 202
Blushing Maiden Supreme, in color, frontispiece
Bouquet Series, 192, 202
Broad mite, 121
Bronze Baby, 192
Bronze Elf, 192
Bronze Girl, 161, 202
Bronze Queen, 185, 202
Burbank, Luther, *Partner of Nature*, 66, 67, 160
Burtt, B. L., 173

C

Calyx, definition of, 234
Canada, imports and exports, 163-164
Capillary attraction, definition of, 234
Christina, 188, 202
Chromosomes, definition of, 234
Classification, by color, 146-149
Cleansing of foliage, 26-27
Clon or clone, definition of, 234
Clorox solution, 131
Colchicine, 66
Color, of saintpaulias, 193
  classification by, 146-149
Color chart, 190-191
Commander, see Commodore
Commercial grower, definition of, 156
Commodore, 138, 147, 156, 206
Compost, definition of, 234
Cordate, definition of, 234

Cox, Harvey, 173, 174, 175
Crenate, definition of, 234
Crock, crocking, definition of, 235
Cross-fertilization, 63-75
  how to record, 76-77
Cross-pollination, definition of, 235
Crown rot, 50, 99-100, 112, 113, 123, 131-132
Crowns, single or multiple, 37-39
Cultural condition, of plant, 157
Curtis Magazine, 170, 181
Cutting, definition of, 235
Cyclamen mite, 97-99, 114-121
  sodium selenate soil treatment for, 118-121

D

Dainty Maid (Pink Lady), 137, 156, 161, 206, 218
Dark Beauty, 63, 185
DDT powder, 10%, 131
Dentate, definition of, 235
Diplotricha B. L. Burtt, species, (formerly S. Kewensis) 148, 173, 175, 176, 178, 179, 182, 206, 222
  description of, 178
  illustration, 177
Disease, and pest, 112-135
Disease control, greenhouse, 93-94, 99-100
Disqualify, definition of, 156
Dithio, 98
Division, multiple-crown, 47-49, 60
Dixie Rose, 19, 206
Double Blue Boy (Double Russian), 149, 192, 202, 206, 208
  illustration, 209
Double Light Blue, 149, 206, 208
Double Neptune, 19, 149, 208
Double Orchid Beauty, 149, 208
Double Russian, see Double Blue Boy
Doubles, 185, 188
Dowfume, 95-96, 125, 130
duPont, Mrs. William K., 188

INDEX

duPont Blue, 138, 208
  illustration, 211
duPont Blue Hybrid, 157, 188, 208
duPont Lavender Pink (duPont Pink), 53, 61, 76, 138, 148, 156, 208
  illustration, 213
  in color, frontispiece
  in color following page 128
  variegated type, illustration, 57
duPont Pink, see duPont Lavender Pink
duPont strain, 19, 51, 63, 67, 76, 185, 188
Dwarf Orchid, 138

E

East African violet, 169-170
Efflorescence disease, 132-134
Eliminate, definition of, 156
Emperor Wilhelm, 161, 208
Endopest, 115, 117, 118, 131
Engler, Adolph, 178
Entire, definition of, 235
Entomology, Bureau of, 96-97
  report on parathion, 96-97
Entry, definition of, 156
Entry cards, African Violet Society, 154
Eva's White, 161
Exhibit, definition of, 156

F

Fantasy, 19, 185, 210
  in color following page 128
Feeding, greenhouse, 91-93
Fermate, 39, 42, 48, 49, 60, 82, 99-100, 105, 107, 132, 134
Fertilizers, 31-33, 45
  commercial, 32
  inorganic, 32
  organic, 32
Fischer's, 92, 99, 192
Flat, definition of, 235
Flower, structure of, illustration, 69
Fluorescent light, 21-22
Foliage, cleansing of, 26-27, 45
Forget-me-not, 148, 208
Formaldehyde dust, 125-126
Frieda, 148, 156, 210
Fringette Series, 185
Fumigation method of soil sterilization, 125-126
Fungous control, 39, 48, 82, 89, 132

G

Gene, definition of, 235
Geneva Rainbow, 63, 210
Genus, genera, definition of, 235
Germination, definition of, 235
Gesneria family, 64, 160, 175
Gloxinias, 64, 169
Goetz, W., 182
Goetzeana, Engler, species, 175, 176, 178, 222
  description of, 178
Gorgeous (Grand Lady), 148, 159-161, 210
Grand Lady, see Gorgeous
Greenhouses, 86-111
  feeding, 91-93, 107
  heating, 88, 103-104, 108
  pest and disease control, 93, 96-100, 106
  shading, 89
  soil sterilization, 94-96, 105, 111-112
  ventilation, 100-102, 106, 108, 110
  watering, 90-91, 105, 110
Greenhouse, hobby, month-by-month suggestions, 103-111
Grooming of plants, 156-157
Grotei, Engler, species, 173-176, 179, 192, 222, 224
  description of, 179
Gypsy Pink, 161
Gypsy group, 161

H

Hand pollination, 68-73
  illustration, 71

241

INDEX

Harvey soil formula, 30
Haworth, James P., *Plant Magic*, 65-67
Heating, of greenhouse, 88
Helen Wilson, *see* Tinari's Helen Wilson
Humidity, 27-29, 45, 101, 102, 104
Humidiguide, 102
Hybrid, definition of, 65, 235
Hybrids, 64-65, 74
Hydroponics, definition of, 235
Hyponex, 31, 35, 50, 82, 92, 105

I

Inorganic fertilizer, definition of, 235
Ionantha H. Wendland, species, 172, 175, 176, 184, 202, 222
  description of, 181
  illustration, 171, 180
  illustration, detail, 225
  spooned type, illustration, 186
Ionantha Grandiflora, 138, 222
Isolation of new plants, 46, 113-114, 130

J

Japanese beetle, 110, 111, 163
Jessie, 195, 196, 212
Judges, saintpaulia shows, 154-155

K

K 6451, 98
Kapsulate, 119

L

Labeling plants, 158
Lacy Girl, 185, 212
Lady Geneva, 63, 159-161, 185, 212
  in color, following page 128
Lady Ulery, 63, 161, 185
Lancaster Red, 161, 222
Larvacide, 94-96, 125, 130
Lath houses, 43
Lavender Lady, *see* Amethyst

Leaf forms, typical, 193
  illustration, 194
Leaf propagation, 39, 47, 49-55, 107, 108
  pot-in-pan method, 55-56
  illustration, 52
  in soil, 54-55
  illustration, 52, 53
  in water, 50-54
  illustration, 52, 53
  variegation, problem of, 56-59
  illustration, 57
Leatherneck strain, 185, 188
Leaves
  wrapping and mailing, 162-163
  illustration, 166, 167
  zoning regulations, 163
Light, 44
  in greenhouse, 104-106
Light Blue Girl, *see* Sailor Girl
Lilac Lady, 148, 214
Liqua-vita, 50

M

Magungensis E. P. Roberts, species, 175, 176, 181-182, 192, 224
  description of, 181-182
Malachite green, 97
Mary Wac, *see* Orchid Beauty
Mauve Fringette
  in color following page 128
Mealy bug, 97-99, 113, 123, 127-128
Medium, definition of, 236
Mendel, Law of Hybrids, 64, 65, 74
Mentor Boy, 19, 46, 70, 138, 148, 214
Mica, *see* Vermiculite
Midrib, definition of, 236
Mildew control, 97, 99
Miniatures, 63, 182, 192
Mites, 28, 38, 46, 97, 100, 104, 108, 112-114, 127
  See also Cyclamen mite
Mrs. Boles, 61, 76, 216
Mulberry Girl, 19, 161, 216

Mutant (variant or sport), definition
   of, 236
Mutation, 58, 64-65, 74
My Lady Series, 161

N

Naegelia species
   N. achemenoides, 64
   N. zebrina, 64
Nematodes, 31, 39, 94, 96, 100, 105,
   112, 114, 122-124, 132, 135
   prevention, 124
   root, 122-124
Neptune, 56, 138, 148, 196, 216
   in color following page 128
   Spooned, 185, 216
      illustration, 187
New plants from old, 47-60
   division, multiple-crown, 47-49, 60
   leaves, rooting of, 47, 49-55
   from seed, see Seed
   from suckers, 47-49, 59, 60
Nitrogen, 32
NNOR, 99, 115, 116, 118, 127, 128,
   130, 131
No. 32, 147, 216
Norseman, 46, 138, 148, 215, 216
   illustration, 215

O

Obovate, definition of, 236
Obtuse, definition of, 236
Ohio State University, 139
OMPA, 118
Optox, 99, 115, 116, 118, 127, 128,
   130
Orbicularis, species, 173, 174
Orchid Beauty (Mary Wac, Plum
   Pink, Trilby), 138, 139, 148,
   192, 196, 216, 229
Orchid Beauty
   detail, illustration, 219
   Hanging-basket type, illustration,
      189
   illustration, 217

Orchid Crinkles, 19
Orchid Flute, 148, 218
Orchid Girl (Red Head Girl), 46,
   161, 188, 218, 220
Orchid Lady, see Amethyst
Organic fertilizer, definition of, 236
Ovate, definition of, 236
Overpot, definition of, 236

P

Packing, for mailing, 162-168
   illustration, 166, 167
Parathion aerosols, 96-97, 115, 124
Peatmoss, 55, 79-81, 132
Pedicel, definition of, 236
Peduncle, definition of, 236
Pest and disease control, 112-135
   greenhouse, 93-94, 96-99
   spraying, 45-46
Pestox, 118
Pestroy, 131
Petiole, definition of, 236
Petiole rot, 132-134
Phosphorus, 32-33
Pinching, definition of, 236
Pink Beauty, 34, 46, 73, 138, 149,
   159-161, 218, 220
   illustration, 221
   in color, frontispiece
   in color following page 128
Pink Girl, 149, 159-161, 188, 218
Pink Lady, see Dainty Maid
Pink Leatherneck, 161, 218
Pink Perfection, see Pink Beauty
Pink Princess, see Pink Beauty
Pink Star, see Star Pink
Pipe cleaners, 134
Pistil, definition of, 237
Pixie, 192
Plant Industry Section, U.S. Depart-
   ment of Agriculture, 96
Plant lice, see Aphids
Plant Patent Law, 160
Plant quarantine, Bureau of, 163

243

Plants
  patented, 159-161
  wrapping for mailing, 165-168
    illustration, 166, 167
Plantfume, 98, 115
Planthion, 98
Plum Pink, *see* Orchid Beauty
Plunge, definition of, 237
Points, scale of, 147
Pollen, definition of, 237
Pollination
  brief guide to, 77
  hand, *see* Hand pollination
Pot-in-pan method of propagation, 55-56
  illustration, 52
Pot sizes, 35-37, 45
Potash, 33
Potbound, definition of, 237
Potting, art of, 39-42
  illustration, 41
Pressure-canner or pressure-cooker method of soil sterilization, 126
Proliferol, 31, 49, 50, 56, 92
Propagating license, where to obtain, 160
Propagation by leaf, *see* Leaf propagation
  by seed, *see* Seed
Protexall, 99
Purple Beauty, 147, 220
Purple Girl, 161, 220
Pusilla Engler, species, 182-183, 224
  description of, 182-183

Q
Quarantine regulations, 110-111

R
Red Bicolor, *see* Bicolor
Red Bird, 148, 220
Red duPont, 148, 206, 220
Red Head, in color, frontispiece, 138, 148, 220
Red Head Girl, *see* Orchid Girl
Red King, 19, 46, 220
  in color following page 128
Red Lands (Redland), 148, 220
Red spider, 131
Red Spoon, *see* Lancaster Red
Registration, of new varieties, 74-76
Repotting a plant, 40-42
  illustration, 41
Rhombic-ovate, definition of, 237
Ring spot, 134-135
Roberts, Evan Paul, 172-174, 175
Roller slats, 89
Root rot, 123
Rootone, 42, 49, 56
Rosette Red, 192, 222
Ruffles, 51, 148, 222
  illustration, 223

S
S-22 Bicolor, 138, 224
Sailor Boy, 138, 148, 157, 196, 222
Sailor Girl, 161, 212, 224
Sailor Girl, Variegated
  in color, following page 128
Saint Paul, Baron Walter von, 170, 179
Saint Paul, Hofsmarschal Baron von, 170
Saintpaulia, species, *see* Species
Saintpaulia club, how to organize, 136-143
Saintpaulia color chart, 190-191
Saintpaulia language, 234-238
Sapphire, 224
  illustration, 226
Sea Queen, 185
Seed, propagation from, 47, 61-85
  cross-pollination, 61-77
  sowing, 79-85, 106, 107
    illustration, 81
  transplanting, 83
Self-fertilization, 68, 70, 74, 76
Sepal, definition of, 237
Serrated, definition of, 237

Shading, of greenhouse, 89
Shell DD (chloropin), 130
Shifting, definition of, 237
Show terms, 156
Shows and judging, 144-158
Shrimpie, 161, 224
Sinus, definition of, 237
Slugs, 104-105, 110
Snow Prince, 19, 46, 161, 224
   in color, cover
Snow Queen, 149, 161, 224
Societies, saintpaulia, 136-143
Sodium selenate, 99, 100, 104, 108, 109, 115-121, 134
   soil treatment for mite, 118-121
   bylaws, 119-121
   Extra Dilute Method, 118-119
Soil
   analysis of, 34
   leaf propagation in, 54-55
   illustration, 52, 53
   mixture, 29-34, 45
   for sowing, 79
   testing, 91-92
Soil Fumigation for Control of Nematodes, 96
Soil sterilization, 31, 45, 125-126
   baking-pan method, 125
   fumigation method, 125
   greenhouse, 94-96
   packaged soil, 126
   pressure-cooker method, 126
Soilene, 130, 131
Soilfume, 96
Species, definition of, 237
Species, saintpaulia, 169-183
   Amaniensis E. P. Roberts, 176, 192, 222
   description of, 176
   Diplotricha B. L. Burtt, 173, 175, 176, 178, 179, 182, 206, 222
   description of, 178
   illustration, 177

Goetzeana, Engler, 175, 176, 178, 222
   description of, 178
Grotei Engler, 173-176, 179, 192, 222, 224
   description of, 179
Ionantha, H. Wendland, 51, 58, 138, 148, 172, 175, 176, 184, 202, 222
   description of, 181
   Grandiflora, 138, 222
   illustration, 171, 180
   illustration, detail, 225
   spooned type, illustration, 186
Magungensis, E. P. Roberts, 175, 176, 181-182, 192, 224
   description of, 181-182
Orbicularis, 173, 174
Pusilla Engler, 182-183, 224
   description of, 182-183
Tongwensis, B. L. Burtt, 173-176, 224
   description of, 183
Spiders, 97
Spooned Neptune, 185, 216
   illustration, 187
Spoonit, 31, 50
Sport, *see* Mutant
Spraying, 45-46, 83-85
Springtail, 123, 130
Stamen, definition of, 238
Star-of-Bethlehem, 161, 185, 224
Star Pink, 161, 220, 224
Starlight (White Waterlily), 161, 224, 230
   illustration, 227
Sterilization of soil, *see* Soil sterilization
Stigma, definition of, 238
Structure of a flower, illustration, 69
Stunt, 121-122
Sub-irrigation, 91, 238
Substitute varieties, 161
Suckers, 38, 47-49, 59, 60

245

INDEX

Sulphur, 48, 49, 60, 97, 132
  dusting, 39, 42
Summer holiday, for house plants, 42-46
Supreme, see Viking
Symmetry, 156
Systemic, definition of, 238
Systox, 118

T

Tear Drop, 192, 224
  in color following page 128
Temperature, 22, 45, 99, 101-104
Terms, definition of (Saintpaulia language), 234-238
Thrip, 114, 118, 129-130
Tinari's America
  in color following page 128
Tinari's Blue Eyes, 138, 148, 156, 183, 198, 224
  illustration, 205
Tinari's Helen Wilson, 192, 210, 228
  in color following page 128
Tinari's Pink Luster, 12, 161
  illustration in color, cover
Tinaris, 12, 58, 92, 192
Tinted Lady, 148, 183, 210, 228
Tongwensis B. L. Burtt, species, 173-176, 224
  description of, 183
Topaz Sapphire, 138, 228
Trace elements, 33
Trilby, see Orchid Beauty
Turning of plants, 44-45
Twinkle Girl, 63, 185, 228

U

Usambara violet, see East African violet

V

Variant, see Mutant
Variegated Leaf Sport, 138
Variegated varieties, 185
Variegation, problems of, 56-59
  illustration, 57
Varieties, 184-231
  complete list of, with synonyms, 195-231
  new, how to register, 74-76
Variety, definition of, 238
Ventilation, 45
  of greenhouse, 100-102
Vermiculite, 29, 49, 54, 55, 60, 79, 80, 102, 132
Viking (Supreme), 19, 53, 61, 147, 157, 185, 193, 224
  illustration, 229
Voilet Beauty, 19, 25, 228
  in color following page 128
Violette, miniatures, 192

W

Water, rooting leaves in, 50-54
  illustration, 52, 53
Water culture in vases, 34-35
Watering, 23-26, 45
  in greenhouse, 90-91
Wendland, Herman, 170, 172
West Coast Amethyst, (Jessie), 148, 195, 228
White fly, 97
White-fringed beetle, 111
White Fringette
  in color following page 128
White Girl, 149, 161, 206, 228
White King, 149, 161, 228
White Lady, 38, 59, 70, 138, 149, 159-161, 228
  illustration, 231
  in color, frontispiece
White Prince, 25, 229
White Queen, 161, 230
White Sister, 161, 230
White Supreme, 149, 230
White Waterlily, see Starlight
Wilcox, Fay, 72, 73, 79

Wright, Alma, 43, 61-62, 101, 102, 138

Y

Yamtox, 99

Yellow saintpaulia, mythical, 63-64, 137

Z

Zoning regulations, 163

CPSIA information can be obtained at www.ICGtesting.com
Printed in the USA
LVOW10s2225100214

373176LV00010B/297/P